MANCHESTER
CITY COUNCIL

T

Please return / renew this item.
_____

Books can be renewed by phone,
internet or Manchester Libraries app.

www.manchester.gov.uk/libraries

Tel: 0161 254 7777

llah

ah

THE HERITAGE OF PETERBOROUGH BRITISH-PAKISTANI COMMUNITY

Copyright © Author Raja Tahir Masood

Published by Raja Tahir Masood

ISBN 978-0-9570333-3-7

E-mail: tahir.masood4@ntlworld.com

The Objectives

1. To support the heritage history of the British-Pakistani community living in Peterborough.

2. To promote community cohesion, encourage greater interaction and participation.

3. To educate the younger members of the British-Pakistani community on their heritage history and to create an awareness amongst the citywide young people.

4. To generate a greater understanding of the British-Pakistani community amongst other Peterborough communities, which would lead to mutual respect, tolerance and harmony.

5. To recognise the contribution of the British-Pakistani community in the development of Peterborough.

6. To promote Peterborough as a welcoming and vibrant city of opportunity for all communities.

My special thanks to The Co-operative Group for their financial support with this project!

The Heritage of the Community

Review

"I am honoured to be requested by Raja Tahir Masood to write a book review on this subject which is close to my heart in my role as the Chief Executive of Peterborough City Council since 2002.

Peterborough has one of the most culturally diverse communities within Britain and has approximately 100 languages spoken throughout the city. Approximately 20% of our population is from a non-British heritage, with one in three coming from an Asian ethnic group.

This book is most interesting to read as it unfolds a story based on personal accounts of community elders and other champions from different backgrounds and heritage. It has some fascinating photographs, which bring memories of the past and evidence the changes we are constantly going through as a modern society in a global village context.

It is important, in modern day society, to have personal accounts of the heritage of our diverse communities and this one of our British-Pakistani community in Peterborough will be a good reference to all generations of the contributions made by the community elders and other members of the community. It also illustrates how other community groups have worked together to achieve a peaceful and cohesive Peterborough.

The story does not end there, of course, and I know that the great work which is being done will continue to make Peterborough a centre of excellence where people from different backgrounds can get on well with each other with the knowledge that they are truly contributing to making Peterborough a great place to live, work and enjoy."

Gillian Beasley
Chief Executive of Peterborough City Council

The Heritage of the Community

Review

This study of the British-Pakistani community in Peterborough manages to provide valuable insights, experiences and narratives. It takes us from the very first settlers born in Pakistan who came to Peterborough in circa 1958 to work predominantly in the brickyards and on the railways through to the third generation of Pakistani-Britons born in Peterborough.

It tracks a group of young men who shed light on what it is like to live in Peterborough when you are of Pakistani and Muslim heritage. It also highlights the policy context surrounding the men's attitudes toward various facets of their lives, including marriage, family, work, Peterborough in general, and the neighbourhoods in which they live.

Muslims comprise the UK's largest religious minority, and are the object of analysis and concern within various policy arenas and popular debates, including immigration, marriage and partner selection, social cohesion and integration. The reader is taken on a journey of a rich and proud heritage and gathers real insight into what half a century of life in Peterborough has and does mean for this particular community.

One can imagine that all minority communities that have settled in Peterborough can relate to the hardships and desires detailed – but full acceptance of this community's contribution to the city seems still to be fully realised.

Yes, there is a difference between what constitutes culture and what constitutes religion and sometimes people's ignorance of the facts can ignite the wrong perceptions but hopefully this book provides the backdrop to enable the reader to understand and appreciate more fully each other's heritage.

We can safely say that having read this book we have learnt more about the Pakistani Peterborian and commend this book to the reader.

June & Vernon Bull – Local Historians and Authors

The Heritage of the Community

Author's Comments

It is my pleasure and an honour to write on the heritage of Peterborough's British-Pakistani community. As far as I am aware, this is the first ever-comprehensive publication of its nature in over 55 years.

All information is based on my knowledge, assessment & understanding of the events and not knowingly altered or influenced nor aims to benefit any individual or organisation.

I have endeavoured to record all-important aspects of the community's heritage, which holds either any significance or relevance to the community. My way forwards and recommendations come from personal analysis.

Every effort is made to ensure that the book is in simple and in plain English, easy to read, for the young people including the creation of sub-headings.

I apologise for the exclusion of women members of the community; however, the truth is my knowledge of women is limited and I am unable to reflect a fair and balanced view or dispense justice without having a greater understanding. Insha'Allah at some point in the future, I could attempt to cover the female contributions.

My special acknowledgement to my late parents Haji Anayat Ali and Azmat Jan for giving me a decent upbringing: providing love, support and enabling me to shape my life to that person I am today!

Finally, I would also like to thank my colleague youth workers namely; Zahid Masaud, Ibrar Ali Khan, Mohammad Riasat, Mohammed Jangher and Kamran Khan for their support with this project.

CHAPTERS

CHAPTERS

Heritage History

Background

The first people to arrive in the UK from the Indian Sub-continent were the Romani people in the 15th century. We also refer to them as Roma or Travellers. They originated from Northern India and began to migrate to Europe and North Africa around the 11th century. Their first recorded presence in the UK was in 1506 in Scotland after they had arrived from Spain.

Early Migration into the UK

After the onset of British Rule in India, the first directly connected people to arrive in the UK dates back to as early as the mid-17th century. They were sailors, army servants or artillery troopers. In 1813, more than 10,000 Indian Lascars were living in Britain. (A lascar was a sailor or militiaman from South Asia). By 1842, 3,000 lascars were visiting the UK every year, and by 1855, there were 12,000 lascars arriving annually in Britain. In 1872 and 1873, some 3,271 Lascars arrived each year in Britain. This increased to a rate of 10,000 to 12,000 every year throughout the late 19th century. From the 17th century interracial marriages were commonplace in Britain between lascars (mostly Bengali Muslim) and indigenous women in areas like Tower Hamlets in London.

Migrant Population

In 1891, 24,037 Lascars were employed on British merchant ships and by the mid-19th century, 40,000 Indian seamen, diplomats, scholars, soldiers, officials, tourists, businesspersons and students came to Britain. By the late 19th and early 20th centuries, the estimated South Asian migrant population in Britain was around 70,000. The South Asian countries include India, Pakistan, Bangladesh, Nepal, Sri Lanka, Bhutan and the Maldives.

Hardships of Mirpuri Community

The first woe for the Mirpuri people came through the British construction of railway lines from Mumbai and Karachi into the interior of the Punjab. Moving goods by rail became cheaper and quicker. Soon after, the once-thriving river trade reduced, resulting in hundreds of Mirpuri boatmen finding themselves out of jobs. At the same time, the long-distance ocean trade was shifting from sail to steam. There was a huge demand for labour for men prepared to work in the hot, dirty and dangerous stokeholds of the new coal-fired steamers. European seamen avoided such jobs and preferred to work on deck. In the 1870s, the former river boatmen were searching for new employment opportunities although, unfamiliar with stoking coal-fired boilers they were prepared to learn which resulted in them acquiring a monopoly of jobs as engine-room stokers on newly built steamships. They sailed out of Karachi and Mumbai to all parts of the globe. They retained this position until the coal-fired ships were finally phased out at the end of the Second World War.

On the eve of World War I, there were 51,616 Lascars in Britain. They earned much less than an equivalent British seaman, a first-class lascar received on average between £4 and £5 a month.

The World Wars

In both World Wars Indian troops played important roles, especially the large number of Muslim soldiers originating from the integral areas that consisted of Pakistan and Kashmir. The Punjabi Muslims were regarded as the backbone of the old Indian Army, known for their reliability as steady dependable men in any task and made up about a third of the British Indian army.

Menin Gate Memorial at Ypres in Belgium

In the First World War, among the recorded dead at the Menin Gate Memorial at Ypres in Belgium are Muhammad Aslam, Abdullah Khan,

The Heritage of the Community

Ahmad Khan, Muhammad Usman and many others with recognisably Muslim names of the Indians who constituted the volunteer force during the First World War, with approximately 400,000 Muslims serving.

Indian Muslim Soldiers in First World War

Khudadad Khan Victoria Cross (VC)

The first Indian-born man awarded the Victoria Cross (VC) was Khudadad Khan. He was born in 1887 in the Village Dabb district of Mianwali in the state of Punjab. When the First World War broke out,

The Heritage of the Community

he joined the Army as a Private and served with the 129th (Duke of Connaught's Own)Baluchis as a machine gunner. In October 1914, his regiment was sent to the front line in France to help exhausted British troops.

The Germans pushed the Baluchis back and all the gunners were killed apart from Khan who was badly wounded. For his bravery in France and his involvement in preventing the German Army reaching vital ports, Khan received the Victoria Cross. He was the first ever Indian-born person to receive this honour. Khan lived until 1971.

During the Second World War, large numbers of young Muslim men from the state of Kashmir and other areas (which now consist of Pakistan) served in the British Indian Army. The recorded number was 832,500 Indian Muslim soldiers in 1945.

These soldiers fought alongside the British Army during the Second World War, particularly in the battle arenas of France, North Africa, Italy and Burma. In all 87,000 Indian army, soldiers were killed according to the Commonwealth War Graves Commission.

In Italy, 5,500 Indian army deaths (including Muslim casualties) are recorded within British India recruitment logs. 122 Soldiers were identified, as under the age of 18 years and amongst those were 90 Muslim including three 15 year olds: Amir Khan from Attock, Gulab Khan from Rawalpindi, and Mian Khan from Kohat.

Abdul Hafiz Victoria Cross (VC)

In the Second World War, a renowned soldier named Abdul Hafiz, born in Kalanaur Village in the Punjab in 1915 and killed in Burma (now called Myanmar) on 6th April 1944. He served with the ninth Jat Regiment of the Indian Army and led an attack against the Japanese forces in the hills north of Imphal. The regiment met with strong resistance from Japanese and Hafiz was wounded by enemy fire, but he still continued to attack enemy positions and killed several of their soldiers. Hafiz was fatally wounded by machine-gun fire from another Japanese position. Later Abdul Hafiz was posthumously awarded the Victoria Cross.

Noor Inayat Khan

In the Second World War, one of the best known Muslim women to play her part was Noor Inayat Khan a Special Operations Executive (SOE). Born on 1st January 1914 in Moscow, her father was the great grandson of the Tipu Sultan of Mysore. On 19th November 1940, she joined the Women's Auxiliary Air Force(WAAF). In November 1942, she was recruited to join F (France) (SOE). On 13th October 1943, the Nazis arrested Noor and she was executed on 13th September 1944, aged 30, having been brutally tortured. Noor is mentioned in Dispatches and was awarded the French Cross of War with a Gold Star and made a Member of the Order of British Empire (MBE) along with posthumously being awarded the George Cross.

Start of Migration from Mirpur

The earliest small-scale migration from the district of Mirpur started in

The Heritage of the Community

19th century and continued during the two World Wars by engine-room stokers. When their ships docked at British seaports, a small minority jumped ships and disappeared into the port cities such as Liverpool, Cardiff and Glasgow. They soon started new lives by marrying indigenous women, survived by selling goods on door-to-door and remained in Britain forever.

Post-War Britain

After the Second World War In Britain a new set of employment opportunities opened up for migrants. Britain's economy set off on what proved to be a long post-war economic expansion (known as the post-war economic boom), and the Golden Age of Capitalism began in the mid 20th century. Whereas after the creation of Pakistan in 1947, unemployment and poverty were high and people were, finding lives a daily struggle and were searching for employment opportunities in as effort to improve their lives. At that period employment, opportunities were very rare in Pakistan.

Traditionally, the inhabitants of Mirpur district were small landowning farmers and were dependent on seasonal crops and livestock, whilst younger men served in the army. Everyone owned their house regardless whether it was two or ten rooms.

Mangla Dam

The proposed Mangla Dam project brought possibly the worst outcome for the residents of Mirpur district. The project resulted in large numbers of inhabitants losing their fertile farming land as well as their homes. People were desperately seeking new employment opportunities anywhere in the world. Britain had an acute shortage of labour in the foundries of the Midlands particularly in the textile mills of Yorkshire and Lancashire.

Economic Migration

Initially, some negotiations took place between the UK government and the government of Pakistan concerning the supply of a migrant workforce to Britain. The discussions broke down when the UK government tried to impose employment contractual restriction with a single employer and this would have resulted in migrants not having the freedom of choice to change their employer.

Enticed by the employment opportunities the first round of direct migration commenced in the 1950s from the towns and villages of the Mirpur district, (Kotli and Bhimber were sub-divisions of the Mirpur district at that time), in Azad Jammu and Kashmir and the villages of Sarai Alamgir and the city of Gujar Khan from the neighbouring Pakistani province of Punjab to the city of Peterborough.

Newly Arrived Migrant Goals

Many of the earliest migrants had difficulties in raising the required finances and often several immediate families pooled their savings to raise sufficient levels of funds, to enable one person to travel to Britain. At that time, migration from Pakistan to the UK was a simple process, whereby agents prepared all the necessary travel documentations for a small fee.

The earliest migration was by young fit and healthy men in their 20's and 30's. Everyone arrived in the UK with the intention of working hard, saving enough funds and returning to their families back in Pakistan. Many had planned goals to set their own small business, build new houses, purchase land or initiate other projects, which would create employment opportunities, generate income and make their lives more comfortable. The reality was that they were living a utopia with no turning back, signifying the start of permanent migration.

Whilst departing from Pakistan, many migrants made a commitment with the other immediate male relations that as soon as they were in a position to financially provide for them, they would assist them to migrate to the UK as well.

Life in Britain

On their arrival into Peterborough, the new migrants were dependent on local residents for their accommodation. The families frequently imposed restrictions on their lodging terms for example; not allowing them to cook or consume spicy food in the houses and their given reasons were the strong smell of spices was off-putting! Today curry is one of the nation's favourite dishes. In addition, often no visitors were permitted into the houses and if any visitor did unexpectedly turned up at the door then, it was expected that the lodger would take him to the nearest café for their discussions.

Being fewer in numbers, the early migrants were often treated as subjects of curiosity by the indigenous population. Every early arrival has a story to share and some were even asked if they washed their faces would the brown colour of their skin also wash off!

Early Difficulties

The early migrants encountered extremely difficult times, mainly due to their limited command of English and communication to sustain their daily life became a barrier as most were either illiterate or had only acquired a basic primary education in Pakistan. However, they were resourceful people and managed to survive by seeking assistance from other community members and assisting members understood their situation and felt obliged to help them. The migrants also found their new British environment as well as the cold climate very different from their small traditional village way of life and warmer weather conditions, which they were familiar with in Pakistan. Every early arrival viewed new opportunities with enthusiasm and a desire to succeed.

A considerable number of early migrants also experienced problems with employment and whilst being out of work their relatives or friends were responsible for providing their board and lodgings without any paybacks. The unemployed also had expectations that their relations or friends would maintain them. Indeed, close relations or friends actively made collective efforts to assist them to find employment. The earliest migrants were resilient people and not deterred by unemployment, many frequently moved from town to town in the hope of securing employment. Most had endured hardships in Pakistan and arrived in Britain with an open flexible mind to accept any paid employment. They had intentions to work hard and achieve good work accomplishments, as many felt insecure about finding alternative employment and high numbers worked for the same employer ranging from a span of 10 to 30 years. All new migrants arrived in the UK with expectations to improve their quality of life.

Priorities

After securing employment, most migrants budgeted to save funds to pay for travelling and other expenses for their immediate relatives in Pakistan to join them in the UK. The supported members were invited at the earliest possible opportunities. I heard stories from the community surviving elders that the early arrival funded several or even 5, 10 or 15 people to come to Britain, they all felt it was their duty to help others. Their arrival enabled the community to grow steadily in population.

Comfort Zone

Once the community had grown in population, a few entrepreneurial members purchased their own dwellings and invited other members of the community to lodge with them. This move was popular with the community and resulted, in some cases, in numbers as high as 25 to 30 occupants in one house and such numbers being an anathema to some of the indigenous population. Many people preferred to live with their other relations and found that community and family links provided them with a comfort zone, which formed an integral part of their lives. It also eased their transition into a new environment and meant that they could live more affordably, save funds and quickly repay their borrowed money, which had enabled them to come to Britain in the first place. The early generation presented themselves as honest, caring, considerate, reliable, flexible, helpful and hard working people.

Family Contact

The earliest arrivals were in regular contact with their families in Pakistan by letters as well as providing them with finances to improve their quality of lives. In Pakistan, their families lived in an extended setup, which included parents, several siblings their families and children. They treated their nephews' and nieces like their own children

Every three to four years almost all migrants visited their families in

Pakistan. The majority of early migrants were married with young children and stayed with their families for several months before returning to Britain. While in Pakistan, almost every one-constructed a new house with updated facilities with their British saved money or others purchased more land. Their peak visiting months were October/November and that was due to the change of climate in Pakistan. There were also a small percentage of single men in the community, who dated local women and in some cases this developed into lasting relationships and they set up homes together and had families.

In the later years, Immigration and Nationality Acts were applied at varying stages to restrict further immigration. Anti-discriminatory laws were approved, aimed at protecting the immigrants already living in UK.

❖ The Commonwealth Immigrants Act 1962

Imposed for the first time was a moderate form of control on Commonwealth citizens, limiting the numbers allowed to enter and seek work through a generous voucher scheme. It also allowed British resident fathers to invite their adult children over (aged 18 or over) to join them in Britain. After the implementation of this Act, a large number of UK settled fathers invited their sons from Pakistan to join them in the UK.

O The Race Relations Act 1965

"The signs of civilisation are to care for the poor, weak, needy and those least able to look after themselves and have laws to protect them" Alexander the Great

This was the first legislation in the UK to address racial discrimination. The Act outlawed discrimination on the "grounds of colour, race, ethnic or national origins" in public places. After UK saw an influx of economic migrants arriving from Commonwealth countries, casual prejudices by colour was a daily part of life in the UK. It also prompted the creation of The Race Relations Board in 1966 to consider complaints under the Act.

Prior to the Race Relations Act 1965, the discrimination against the minority communities was widespread Signs were often displayed at prominent places stating "No Blacks, No Dogs and No Irish". Blacks and Irish were counted in the same category as the dogs. This legislation was considered long overdue for the black and minority people living in Britain

Enoch Powell Speech

On Saturday 20th April 1968, Enoch Powell, a Conservative Member of Parliament (MP) for Wolverhampton South West, made a speech at 2.30 p.m. in the Midland Hotel in which he highlighted the issue of immigration in his now-famous 'Rivers of Blood' speech. He warned his audience of what he believed would be the consequences of continual unchecked immigration from the Commonwealth to Britain and highlighted the proposed anti-discrimination legislation.

The speech caused a huge political storm making Powell one of the most popular, though divisive, politicians in the country which led to his dismissal from the Shadow Cabinet by Conservative party leader Edward Heath. The speech had a massive impact on the British public and from an historical perspective remains one of the most talked about speeches on immigration.

O The Race Relations Act 1968

This Act made it illegal to refuse housing, employment, or public services to a person on the grounds of colour, race, ethnic or national origins. It also created the Community Relations Commission to promote 'harmonious community relations'.

❖ The Commonwealth Immigration Act 1968

The Commonwealth Immigration Act 1968 introduced annual quotas on East African Asians who had been given UK passports. In 1969, the Labour government additionally required persons seeking to enter as dependents from Pakistan, to seek 'entry clearance'. This Act only allowed dependents into the UK and that meant wives and children.

This Act was the start of the interview process at the British High Commission Offices in Pakistan. It also meant only dependants were allowed to enter into the UK with little deviation. The married men started to invite their families to join them. A large number of dependent women and children arrived to start family lives in the UK.

❖ The Immigration Act 1971

This Act described by the Government as a 'firm but fair' immigration policy, intended to 'control immigration from all sources on the same basis', was viewed as an essential prerequisite for satisfactory race relations. Its explicit aim was to limit immigration from Commonwealth and foreign countries on the same defensible footing. It abolished special quotas and other distinctions that Commonwealth subjects had enjoyed over foreign citizens. It also established the same procedure for labour migration, based on work permits for all migrants.

From 1977, newly married husbands were no longer being accepted for settlement on arrival, but instead were given 'limited leave to enter.' This was intended to reduce illegal immigration through bogus 'marriages of convenience'. This change affected some women members of the community who decided to return to Pakistan to get married.

O The Race Relations Act 1976

This Act was probably the most comprehensive Act of Parliament of its time and its aim was to prevent discrimination based on race. It covered discrimination on the grounds of race, colour, and nationality, ethnic and national origin in the field of employment, the provision of goods and services, education and public functions. The Act also established the Commission for Racial Equality with a remit to review the legislation, which was put in place to make sure the Act and its regulations were followed.

❖ British Nationality Act 1981

This Act came into force on 1st January 1983 and set out a definition as to who is classed as British and how people can become British citizens through naturalisation. The vast majority of migrants from Pakistan who were eligible for naturalisation did apply and benefited by becoming dual UK and Pakistani nationals, although the fees were expensive for the low paid. After being awarded British naturalization citizenship, many members of the community were euphoric with thoughts that at last the British government had recognised their many decades of contributions to the British economy.

Each of the above Acts further restricted primary immigration although family members of already settled migrants were allowed to join their relatives.

O Race Relations Amendment Act 2000

The Race Relations Amendment Act 2000 places a duty on most public authorities to eliminate race discrimination, promote equality of opportunity and good relations between all racial groups. The aim being to promote racial equality by helping public authorities provide fair and accessible services and in addition improve and provide equal employment opportunities for all racial groups. The two major components of the legislative framework is to assist public authorities in complying with their new obligations, as introduced by the Race Relations Amendment Act 2000, and are what are known as the 'general duty' and the 'specific duties'. The recent Acts that apply to a small section of the British- Pakistani community are:

O Citizenship ceremonies for all new applicants to British citizenship from 1st January 2004. Applicants who are aged 18 or over are required to attend a citizenship ceremony and take an Oath of Allegiance and a Pledge to the UK before their grant of British citizenship can take effect.
O The "Life in the UK" test must be passed before an application is made to the Home Office. Those who pass the test do not need to provide separate evidence of language competence.
O The Immigration, Asylum and Nationality Act 2006, is a UK Act of Parliament, which came into effect on 30 March 2006.

O The Racial and Religious Hatred Act 2006

This Act of Parliament created an offence in England and Wales of inciting hatred against a person on the grounds of their religion.

O The Act amends the Public Order Act 1986 by creating new offences of stirring up hatred against persons on religious grounds and amends section 24A of the Police and Criminal Evidence Act (PACE) 1984 so that the powers of citizens' arrest do not apply to the offences of stirring up religious or racial hatred.
O The new offences apply to the use of words or behaviour or display of written material, publishing or distributing written material, the public performance of a play, distributing, showing or playing a recording, broadcasting or including a programme in a programme service and the possession of written materials with a view to display, publication, distribution or inclusion in a programme service or the possession of

recordings with a view to distribution, showing, playing or inclusion in a programme service.

O For each offence the words, behaviour, written material, recordings or programmes must be threatening and intended to stir up religious hatred. Religious hatred is defined as hatred against a group of persons defined by reference to religious belief or lack of religious belief.

Today the British-Pakistani is a well-established community with a majority British born population. Unfortunately, the overwhelming members of the community ignore the English language, which is another major cause of concern.

❖ Introduced Compulsory Language Tests from 2010

■ The UK Government introduced compulsory English language tests in autumn 2010 for non-European Union migrants applying for a UK visa to come to the UK to join or marry their settled partner.

■ The changes mean partners will need to demonstrate that they have a basic command of English before leaving Pakistan, around the level of a five- to seven-year-old, which will allow them to cope with everyday life in the UK. The new test assesses a person's ability to introduce themselves, ask simple directions, and understand what someone speaking slowly says.

■ While a seemingly uncontroversial UK immigration requirement for new migrants, it also seems an unnecessary law given that the UK already requires migrants to speak English. Partners who have completed the initial two-year period of temporary residence still need to pass the "Knowledge of Language and Life in the UK" test before obtaining permanent residence.

■ The Home Office has acknowledged that the people most likely to be adversely affected are those coming from Pakistan, where English is not spoken in rural areas or by poor or illiterate people.

■ There will be certain applicants who will struggle to pass the tests, which could mean long delays before they can join their partners in UK. In some cases and even for those who do pass the test, having to sit the test will mean an extra step and fee to pay, as well as the time and effort involved.

■ The Home Office estimates the new law will lead to a drop of around 10% in UK visa applications.

We will have to await the outcome on how these new requirements will affect spouses of the British-Pakistani person marrying in Pakistan andwhether the drop in visa applications actually happens.

Recent Migration

There are still Pakistani migrants arriving in Britain today taken from a recent report, below are the reasons for migration to the UK.

- Study
- Joining a family member
- Gaining life experience
- Marriage
- Work

The work permit visas tend to be for highly skilled professionals such as doctors and other health professionals. Since 1999, there has been a significant increase in the number of grants of settlement given to Pakistanis. Between 1991 and 1998 grants of settlement averaged 6,400 per year, but since 1999 they averaged 11,300 per year.

Areas of Heritage

The heritage areas of the Peterborough's British-Pakistani community consist of the Mirpur district, the town of Sarai Alamgir, Kotli district, Gujar Khan city and the Bhimber district.

Mirpur, Kotli and Bhimber districts are all in Azad Jammu and Kashmir (Free Kashmir) and Sarai Alamgir and the Gujar Khan are located in Northern Punjab, adjacent to Azad Jammu and Kashmir. The majority of Peterborough's British-Pakistani come from the Mirpur district, towns and villages of:

- Islamgarh,
- Kakra town
- Ibrahimabad
- Kalyal Bainsi
- Potha Bainsi
- Kaneli
- Mirpur city
- Khari Sharif

Islamgarh (formerly Akalgarh) is a well-established town where a high population of British-Pakistani, are now residing in Peterborough. Most are either are related or know each other's families well. The small inhabitants of Indian controlled Kashmir and migrated to Azad Jammu and Kashmir in 1947. The earliest migrants to arrive in Peterborough from the Mirpur district were around 1957.

The second largest migrant community to settle in Peterborough came from the villages around the town of Sarai Alamgir in Northern Punjab. Most people are related to each other or know one another fully.

The Sarai Alamgir members of the community arrived in Peterborough around 1957. They all came from four closely located villages namely:

- Orangabad
- Chapper
- Kotian
- Nathyan

The third largest migrant community came from the district of Kotli, around the towns and the villages of:

- Kala Dab,
- Charhoi,
- Dhamal,
- Khanka Katara
- Damass
- Chack
- Juna
- Khuiratta
- Sarhi
- Nara Koot
- Chaflotti
- Kotli city

The Kotli migrants came from widespread areas all over the Kotli district. The Kotli migrants were amongst the earliest to arrive in Peterborough around 1956.

The next two largest members of the Peterborough British-Pakistani community come from Gujar Khan city and surrounding villages in Northern Punjab and the villages of the Bhimber district in Azad Jammu and Kashmir. Both members of the communities first arrived in Peterborough in 1960s.

One of those communities came from the well-known village of Ladiyah It is a small village located near the town of Kotla in the district of Gujrat (Punjab).

Peterborough has small numbers of families originating from the cities of Lahore, Faisalabad, Jhelum, Attock, Pindi, Gujranwala and from the towns of Dina, Kala Gujran, Jalalpur Jattan and from other Punjab province towns and cities.

The remaining members of British-Pakistani community resident in Peterborough come from the former Mangla Dam affected areas of Mirpur district, who are now resettled mainly around the city of Faisalabad, towns of Joharabad and Mandi Bahauddin as well as in several other small towns and villages in the Pakistani province of Punjab.

Facts about Pakistan

I have included these facts to give you a greater understanding of Pakistan. The name Pakistan means Land of (the) Pure in Urdu and Persian.

The official name of the country is the Islamic Republic of Pakistan and Pakistan means land of pure. It is located in South Asia.

The country gained its Independence on 14th August 1947 from the UK and the founding leader was Quaid-e-Azam Muhammad Ali Jinnah.

The country motto is Unity, Discipline and Faith and its currency is Pakistani Rupees. Pakistan capital is Islamabad and Karachi is the largest city in the country.

The country consists of four provinces namely Punjab, Sindh, Balochistan and Khyber Pakhtunkhwa, Pakistan's population is about 177 million and it is the second most populous Muslim country after Indonesia and the sixth most populous country in the world.

Pakistan land area is 796,095 km and the country has borders with India, Iran, Afghanistan and China.

The Indus region, which covers a considerable amount of Pakistan, was the site of several ancient cultures and Indus Valley Civilisation (2500–1500 BCE) at Harappa and Mohenjo-Daro.

The country official language is Urdu it is also widely spoken language in the neighbouring country India. The term 'Urdu' is a Turkish word, which means army. It is estimated that over 400 million people worldwide speak Urdu.

It is estimated that seven million Pakistanis now live abroad and three of their largest overseas communities are in UK, Saudi Arabia and the United Arab Emirates.

Pakistan arm forces are the eighth largest in the world with over six hundred thousand regular and about five hundred thousand reserves troops. It is the first and the only Islamic nuclear power country in the world.

Mirpur

Background

Old Mirpur city was founded in 1052 AH (around 1642 AD) by a Chief called Miran Shah Ghazi (whose ancestors migrated from Mashhad in Iran to Kashmir) and Sultan Fateh Khan.

Between 1831 and 1839, Ranjit Singh bestowed Gulab Singh the royalties of the salt mines in Northern Punjab, and handed the control of the Northern Punjab towns of Mirpur, Jhelum, Gujrat and Rohtas. Gulab Singh continued expanding his kingdom and in 1840, Baltistan was made subject to Jammu. Gilgit fell to a Sikh force from Kashmir in 1842. Ranjit Singh annexed the state of Kashmir in 1819. However, the rebellion in Hazara at the beginning of 1846 compelled the country to be transferred to Raja Gulab Singh of Jammu.

The aftermath of the first Anglo Sikh War resulted in the Treaty of Lahore to be signed on 9th March 1846 between the British Government and Raja Gulab Singh of Jammu and the birth of the Treaty of Amritsar came about on 16th March 1846. The British Government sold Kashmir to the Raja of Jammu for 75 million rupees. The area included eastward of the River Indus and westward of the River Ravi including Chamba and excluding Lahul. This Treaty transferred to him all the hill states including the Kashmir Valley and Hazara thus sealing the fate of Mirpur with the new state of Jammu and Kashmir. Raja Gulab Singh became the Maharaja of the Princely state of Jammu and Kashmir. He imposed severe taxations to recoup his money including the annual land tax, which brought resentment and further hardships on already impoverished citizens of the state.

The citizens of Jammu and Kashmir were overwhelmingly Muslim and their Dogra ruler was a Sikh, which brought constant tension between the subjects and their ruler.

In 1947, the British granted independence to Pakistan. The Kashmiri people revolted against their Dogra ruler of state and this led to a campaign for a free Kashmir. Their struggle went on for several months before the Dogra ruler was defeated by the Kashmir Liberation Army on 24th October 1947, where a provisional government of Azad Jammu and Kashmir (Free Kashmir) was established.

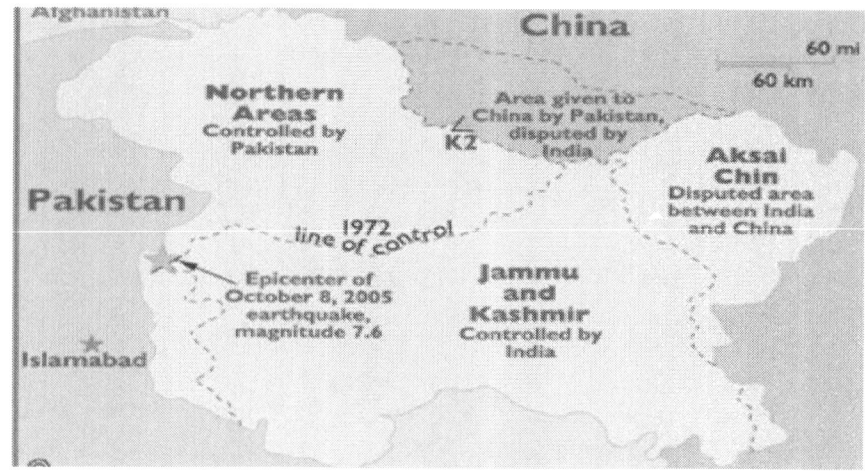

Jammu and Kashmir

Prior to the 1947 partition, Hindu and the Sikh families who were resident in Mirpur city owned almost all of the businesses. Hindus & Sikhs populated the district, but the overwhelming majority of the population were Muslims in the surrounding small towns and villages. In 1947 when Kashmir freedom campaign started and because of Mirpur location and established city status, it became an assembly for Hindus and Sikhs families living in the neighbouring cities, towns and villages, including from the adjacent Pakistani areas before vacating the city and heading towards the city of Jammu.

Nanga Parbat in Kashmir, Pakistan

Muslims from the Indian controlled Kashmir also fled to the Azad Jammu and Kashmir area in equal or even greater numbers. The mass migration of people was a two way process resulting in terrible suffering for common people.

Mangla Dam

Amongst the complications in the Mangla Dam's proposed project was that the old city of Mirpur was located under the Dam water area and without a choice the city had to relocate. The old Mirpur city was only five kilometres from the town of Islamgarh and the initial decision reached was to relocate the new Mirpur city on the Eastern hills of Islamgarh. The local residents fiercely opposed the plan and felt that by becoming part of the new Mirpur city their small traditional town culture and ways of life could be eroded or even disappear forever.

After Islamgarh's refusal to accept the new city proposal, the present location was identified as the best alternative and the new Mirpur city was built on the nearby banks of Mangla Dam in the late 1960's. Old Mirpur

Falaksair Peak in swat valley in Kashmir, Pakistan

Today the remains of old Mirpur city are underneath the water of the Mangla Dam. At that time of disbanding the old city almost every building apart from the religious worshiping buildings were dismantled. Even now during the winter months, when the Dam's water recedes, the minarets of the old Mirpur city mosques, remnants of a Sikh gurdwara and a Hindu temple become visible from a distance. This is a glimpse of communities belonging to all religions, where people lived together in the city before the partition of Indian Sub-continent.

New Mirpur

The new Mirpur city is located at 459 metres above sea level. Lying between 33°15' and 33°34' latitude, and 73°31' and 73°55' longitude, and is located at the far South of Azad Jammu and Kashmir.

Mirpur is the largest city in Azad Jammu and Kashmir. It is located 129 kilometres east of the Pakistan capital Islamabad and 254 kilometres south of the Azad Jammu and Kashmir capital Muzaffarabad.

New Mirpur city was well planned with a good infrastructure and all buildings are of a modern design. The city has expensive residential dwellings, which come in a variety of shapes and sizes. The headquarters of Mirpur district comprises of three sub-divisions;

- Mirpur city
- Dadyal
- Chakswari

Dadyal is 65 kilometres North from Mirpur city and consists of about 70 villages with population of 40,000. A large Dadyal population is now living in the UK, mainly in towns and cities of the Midlands. They were amongst the earliest migrants to arrive in the UK.

Chowk Shaheedan in Mirpur city centre

The Heritage of the Community

Chakswari is located on the road connecting Mirpur with Kotli. It is 40 kilometres from Mirpur city with a population of 20,000 and is fast becoming a commercial area. A large Chakswari population is also now residing in the UK.

Towns

Mirpur district's main town is Islamgarh. The town is 30 kilometres from the city of Mirpur and located on the road connecting Mirpur with Kotli on fertile land. It is a well-established town with a population of 18,000 and is estimated that two-thirds of the Islamgarh and surrounding village population is now settled in the UK.

The other small towns in the Mirpur district are Mangla, Khari Sharif, Kakra town and Ibrahimabad.

Mangla is a beautiful modern town 16 kilometres from the city of Mirpur and located at the mouth of the Mangla Dam. The construction of the Dam has turned the town into an exciting place. The town has thesecond largest power station in Pakistan.

Cricket Stadium in Mirpur

Khari Sharif is located 8 kilometres from Mirpur city. It's a town is known for housing the Shrine of the Sufi Saint known as Baba Pir-e-Shah Ghazi (Damrian Wali Sarkar). Also, at Khari Sharif is the Shrine of the late Mian Mohammed Baksh, a Sufi Saint and a Punjabi Pothohari poet. He is especially renowned for writing a book of poetry called Saif-ul Maluk and it is a well-known book all over in Northern Pakistan. Saif-ul Maluk Festival is held annually in April at the Khari Sharif.

New Kakra town was re-built in 1960s as the Mangla Dam waters engulfed the old Kakra village. The residents of old Kakra either moved to new Kakra town or resettled in several areas in the Pakistani province of Punjab. A sizeable Kakra town population is now living in Peterborough.

Ibrahimabad is amongst the fastest growing small town in the Mirpur district. It was founded in mid 1970's by my maternal grandfather late Haji Mohammed Ibrahim. In the last 35 years, some of the districts most modern dwellings are constructed around this town. A large population from the surrounding villages are also now living in Peterborough including people of my birth village of Morah Bari.

Regency Hotel in Mirpur

Benefits of Migration

The result of mass migrations from Mirpur district currently accounts for about 60-70% of the Pakistanis living in Britain originated from this one small district. Mirpur has one of the highest inflation figures in Pakistan this is due to the significant investment from expatriates now living in the UK and in other worldwide countries.

The residents of Mirpur live in harmony and with real community spirits

The Heritage of the Community

where wealthy people view themselves as privileged, as many are humbled by the reminders about their pastimes, and most take care of other poor and the needy people.

The large-scale migration from Mirpur district in the last half of the 20th century means that today the Mirpuri people are living in almost every continent in the world and representing the Kashmiri community.

Mirpuri Culture

Despite their wealth and large population living abroad, the Mirpur district remains a conservative society even by Pakistani standards. Life in its rural villages continues to be dominated by rigid hierarchies and families tend to be close knit. The Mirpuri community has a strong emphasis on retaining their Punjabi Pothohary language, conservative culture, values and traditions, especially by those who have now migrated and are living abroad.

A village in Mirpur district

Establishments and British Influence

Mirpur has a large number of private education establishments including primary, secondary schools to universities, hospitals, hotels, restaurants, shopping malls and all other urban facilities required for a modern city of this size to function effectively. Over five decades of strong connections with Britain has resulted in many establishments being named after British companies, towns and cities as Mirpur is inexorably influenced by British culture.

Opportunities

The newfound wealth from expatriates has made Mirpur a vibrant and thriving business and enterprise hub, creating opportunities for other residents of the city, those from Kashmir and Pakistan at large.

British Friendship Links

A considerable Mirpuri population is now settled in the UK and their continuous endeavours are to retain the strong cultural and traditional links with Mirpur. Indeed, many of their newly adopted British cities have established friendship links with Mirpur city namely:

- o Birmingham
- o Bradford
- o London Borough of Waltham Forest

Monument of Basharat shaheed in Mirpur

Tourist Attractions

Mirpur has many tourist attractions and interesting places to visit in and around the city. These include: Basharat Shaheed Monument, Jari Kas, Mangla Dam, Mangla Fort and Museum, Ramkot Fort and Khari Sharif - eight kilometer.

The Makeup of the Present Mirpuri Population

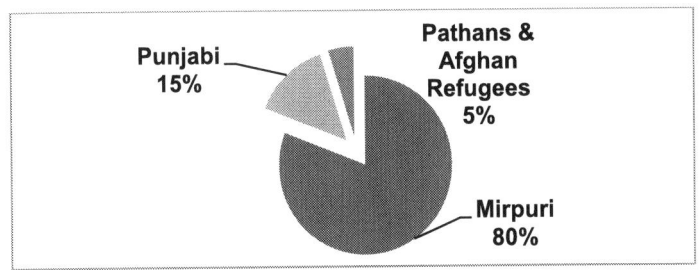

Distances from Mirpur City

Mirpur	Islamgarh	30 Kilometres
Mirpur	Chakswari	40 Kilometres
Mirpur	Bhimber	50 Kilometres
Mirpur	Saria Alamgir	50 Kilometres
Mirpur	Dadyal	65 Kilometres
Mirpur	Gujar Khan	70 Kilometres
Mirpur	Kotli	101 Kilometres
Mirpur	Islamabad	129 Kilometres
Mirpur	Lahore	216 Kilometres
Mirpur	Muzaffarabad	254 Kilometres
Mirpur	Peshawar	303 Kilometres
Mirpur	Quetta	945 Kilometres
Mirpur	Karachi	1493 Kilometres
Mirpur	Peterborough	6040 Kilometres

Kotli District

Background

Kotli was founded about 500 years ago. Prior to this, the area was covered in dense forests. The Kotli district was a sub-division of the Mirpur district until 1975 and known as Kotli Mangralan. It has beautiful views of valleys and hills that rise gradually towards the high mountains of the Poonch district.

The Kotli district population is estimated to be 650,000. In the early days, the name Kotli originated from the locally spoken language being koh and talay which together mean 'a population under mountains'. With time, it evolved into the present day name of Kotli and it has five sub-divisions namely:

1. Kotli city
2. Fatehpur Thakiala or Naykal
3. Sehnsa
4. Khuiratta
5. Charhoi

Naykal is renamed Fatehpur Thakiala to honour the late Sardar Fateh Muhammad Khan Karelvi. It is a small town located in a magnificent valley about three kilometres from the Line of Control (LOC) Fatehpur Thakiala and its surrounding areas are considered amongst the most beautiful parts of Azad Jammu and Kashmir. The town is 40 kilometres from Kotli city.

Khuiratta is also known as Wadi-e-Bnah. Khuiratta and its surroundings are popular among tourists and only 8 kilometres from LOC. It is famous for its colourful mela (festival) known as the Baisakhi Mela. During the mela, 1000's of people gather from all over the country to view its many attractions, this mela is exclusive to Khuiratta in Azad Jammu and Kashmir and it lasts for three days with activities including bull racing, wrestling, weight lifting, kabaddi, volleyball, football, live music and other forms of traditional entertainment.

At about a distance of four kilometres from Khuiratta is the famous shrine of "Mai Totti Sahiba Darbar" A crowd of people visits the shrine every day.

Sehnsa is located at a distance of 35 kilometres from Kotli. Nearby is the scenic and beautiful Bruhian, which is surrounded by forests.

A village in Kotli district

Gulpur town is another Kotli district town. It is located at the junction of the Kotli-Mirpur and Kotli-Rawalpindi road. Adjoining Gulpur town is Throtchi, renowned for its castle built in 1460. It was in Gulpir in 1947 that a contingent of local men headed by Col Mahmood besieged the Dogra army soldiers at the Throtchi Castle until they decided to retreat for Jammu.

British Friendship Links

A large population from the Kotli district have migrated to the UK and because of the heritage links, their newly adopted hometowns or cities have established cultural and friendship links with Kotli. The British cities and towns with friendship links are:

o Birmingham
o Bradford
o Luton
o Rochdale
o Sheffield

General Information

Kotli is also known as the city of mosques, there are more than 300 mosques.

At a distance of 26 kilometres from Kotli city lies Tattapani (hot water) a popular mythical destination where thousands of people flock to the Sulphur Springs each year in the hope of finding magical cures for illnesses.

Kotli district

Minar-e-Pakistan in Lahore, built in commemoration of the Pakistan Resolution on 23rd March 1940 Construction started in 1960 and completed in 1968

Sarai Alamgir Town

Sarai Alamgir is a large town and a sub-division of the Gujarat district with a population of about 190,000. The town is located at a historic crossroads between the ancient Grand Trunk Road and the Jhelum River, with only a short trip from Jhelum.

The ancient history of the region has seen several early civilizations including the Indus Valley. Nearby, the Battle of the Hydaspes took place between the armies of Alexander the Great and the Great King Porus.

Sarai was founded by the Mughal Emperor Aurangzeb because of its strategic location on the Grand Trunk Road and the Jhelum River, as well as its proximity to Kashmir. Over time, the Sarai developed into a convenient town for the adjoining village Community. In olden days, people of influence would build a Sarai (caravan stations and rest houses) for travellers. A typical Sarai would consist of a drinking well and a praying area along with a sleeping place for people.

The town gained prominence in 1922 when the British established a military school. It was one of four such cadet schools in British India to benefit the sons of members of the Royal Indian Army. The college is now known as the Military College Jhelum. The town possesses good transport links including a railway station.

Faisal Mosque in Islamabad is the largest mosque in Pakistan named after the late King Faisal of Saudi Arabia and completed in 1986

The Heritage of the Community

Bhimber District

Bhimber district is located near the border of the Line of Control, between Indian controlled Kashmir and Azad Jammu and Kashmir. Historically, Mughal Kings and other royal families used this route to Srinagar for holidays. Parts of Bhimber district especially Northern parts are mountainous and Southern parts from Bhimber to Barnalah and Koat Jaimel are rather plain with a road that has residential population on both sides.

Bhimber was a sub-division of Mirpur district until 1996 when it became a separate district. The population of Bhimber district is approximately 350,000. Bhimber has three sub-divisions:

- ◆ Bhimber city
- ◆ Samahni
- ◆ Barnalah

Samahni has an estimated population of 120,000 people and the valley is approximately 35 kilometres long and 8 kilometres wide, stretching from Chawlian to Behmla in the West. It is located 17 kilometres to the North of Bhimber city. One of the popular tourist attractions is the Lake Baghsar in Samahni. The lake is located at 975 meters above sea level. The lake is approximately half a kilometre long and overlooks the Bandala Valley.

Barnala area is mainly comprises of foothill, plain and starches land. It is located on the extreme East side of Azad Jammu & Kashmir over the LOC.

It is the famous destination and business market of Bhimber district. Barnala consists of seven union councils and has a total population 110.00 people.

Barnala is connected with Mirpur, Bhimber, Gujarat, Kharian and Sialkot. Barnala is located 46 Kilometres from Gujarat and 200 Kilometres from Rawalpindi.

The famous route to the Jammu city is Kashmir Highway that passes through Barnala. The small towns Kadhala, Barnala, Kot Jamel, Moil, Chumb and Iftikharabad are located on this famous route.

Sarai Alamgir

Bhimber district

The Heritage of the Community

Gujar Khan City

Background

The place was named after Gujjars, who formerly ruled the Gurjara Pratihara Kingdom for centuries.

Location

Gujar Khan city is located on the Islamabad-Lahore National Highway. The city is a sub-division of the Rawalpindi district. The city population is approximately 75,000. It is located about 59 kilometres from the Pakistan capital Islamabad and 2 kilometres from the Dohngi Dam.

Gujar Khan

Pothohar Culture

Gujar Khan lies at the heart of the Pothohar cultural region. Pothohar is on a plateau in Punjab and Kashmir. The area was the home of the Soan Culture, which is evidenced by the discovery of fossils, tools, coins, and the remains of ancient archaeological sites. The local people speak a distinctive dialect of Punjabi.

The Indus Valley civilisation is known to have flourished in the same region between the 23rd and 18th centuries BC. Some of the earliest

Stone Age artefacts in the world have been found on the plateau, dating from 500,000 to 100,000 years.

The Stone Age people produced their equipment in a sufficiently homogenous way to justify their grouping. Around 3000 BC, small village communities developed in the Pothohar area, which led to the early roots of civilization. The Potohar Plateau lies between the Indus River on the west and the Jhelum River on the east. The Margalla Hills and the Kala Chitta Range from its Northern boundary. The Southern boundary is the Salt Ranges. The Swaan River starts from nearby Murree and ends at nearby Kalabagh on the Indus River. The modern day cities of Islamabad and Rawalpindi sit on the plateau.

Friendship Links

A large number of residents from the city have migrated abroad and through their connections; Gujar Khan is twinned with four worldwide cities:

- o Redditch in England
- o Taif in Saudi Arabia
- o Munich in Germany
- o Auckland in New Zealand

The Badshahi Mosque in Lahore, commissioned by the Mughal Emperor Aurangzeb completed in 1673, is the 2nd largest mosque in Pakistan and the 5th largest mosque in the world.

The Heritage of the Community

Mangla Dam

Background

The Mangla Dam project was initially developed in the 1950s as a multipurpose project to be constructed at Mangla. However, the signing of the Indus Water Treaty in 1960 under the sponsorship of the World Bank, assigned the three Eastern Rivers of Ravi, Beas and Sutlej to India and the three Western rivers Indus, Jhelum and Chenab to Pakistan - forming the development of the Mangla Dam.

The Mangla Dam project was one of the largest in the world. The work commenced in 1961 and was completed in 1967. The Mangla Dam was constructed across the Jhelum River in Mirpur district.

Mangla Dam

Displacement

The Mangla Dam was the biggest modern peacetime project to have a radical impact on the lives of a large population of Mirpur district. The building of the original Dam:

O Displaced 110,000 people
O 280 villages were uprooted and lost

The building of the Mangla Dam uprooted established communities in

The Heritage of the Community

the Mirpur district. It forced people to vacate their homes and ancestral land. The displaced people paid a heavy price, as they were resettled 100's of kilometres away in new undeveloped and often remote rural areas in the province of Punjab in Pakistan. The Dam affected the local well-established communities, and in majority of cases, close-knit families were divided. It was the luck of the draw depending on where your village was located and often half of their unaffected family members were left behind. The displaced people had to make a fresh start the hurdles being living a new environment, divided families and occasionally problematic times from the local people of the areas.

Purpose

The purpose of the Mangla Dam was to conserve and control the floodwater of the Jhelum River through a significant reduction in flood peaks and volumes downstream. This was achieved partly through incidental use of the available storage space. Other reasons for the dam included power generation to meet electricity demands; the plentiful supply of fish to meet the country's rich diet; and to provide healthy recreation facilities for both local people and tourists.

Specifications

The Mangla Dam is 3,140 metres long and 138 metres high with a reservoir of 253 square kilometres. The main spillway consists of nine concrete gates 36'x40' capable of passing a peak flood of 870,000 cusecs at a maximum conservation level of 366 metres. The second spillway is located in Jari Kas about 27 kilometres from the Main Dam with a maximum height of 80 metres.

Second Phase

The work is in progress on the second phase on Mangla Dam, in order to remedy the decreasing storage capacity. The government of Pakistan has decided to raise the Dam by 10 metres. This will increase the Dam capacity by 18% and sadly displace a further:

♦ 43,000 people
♦ 113 villages

The government is making payments to those affected by this extension and has earmarked the compensatory amount of 35 billion rupees. On this occasion, the affected people are reluctant to resettle 100's of kilometres away, which has forced the government to establish nearby partnership-developed resettlement areas by the Pakistani and Chinese companies in;

> ➤ Mirpur city
> ➤ Chakswari
> ➤ Siakh
> ➤ Dadyal
> ➤ Islamgarh

Mangla Park

The Bridge

Another new exciting project under construction is a bridge linking Mirpur city with the town of Islamgarh via the Mangla Dam. The bridge is called the "Rotha Hariam Bridge". Once the work is completed and the bridge is opened it will reduce the travelling time and the distance between Mirpur city and the town of Islamgarh to approximately 7-9 kilometres from the current 30 kilometres. The bridge will also reduce the travelling time and distance between Mirpur city and its sub-division towns of Chakswari and Dadyal, as both towns' access roads are via Islamgarh town. In the long term, this project will bring huge economic benefits for the residents of the Mirpur district and the people of Azad Jammu and Kashmir.

Peterborough Heritage

Introduction

Peterborough is a historic, industrial, multicultural, modern, desirable, tolerant city to live and work. It is one of the fastest growing cities in the UK with excellent road and rail links. It enjoys being a commuter city, which has a high number of diverse communities and continues to welcome new arrivals.

Peterborough is more than a collection of buildings of offices, shops and civic centres. It is a place where people engage in recreation, work and live. It has a long and proud history from the Jurassic through Neolithic, Bronze, Roman, Anglo-Saxon, Mediaeval, Tudor, Georgian and Victorian to the present twenty first century. Peterborough was given the city status on the 4th of September 1541.

In more recent times Peterborough has gone from a rural small sleepy city to a vibrant city, and changes in the city's social history, political development, local government and religious influence has brought progress and an improved quality of life.

Peterborough owes its origins to the establishment of a Celtic monastery in about 655, but only in Victorian times did the city begin to grow outside its medieval streets, mainly due to its new role as a railway centre.

Today, the city continues to expand in the new millennium as a regional centre for homes, commerce, transport, industry and leisure.

City Location

Peterborough is located approximately 121 kilometres North of London. The city stands transversely on the river Nene and is bordered by Cambridgeshire, Northamptonshire and Lincolnshire. It is located in North Cambridgeshire in the East of England.

Background

Peterborough's rich history is highlighted in the summary below. All the main historic and significant events are recorded chronologically.

43AD: the Romans established the fortified garrison town of Durobrivae on Ermine Street, about five miles west of present-day Peterborough.

655: a monastery dedicated to St Peter was founded here. **972:** an abbey was built.

1086: Peterborough was recorded in the Domesday Book.

1117: the abbey was destroyed by fire.

1118: the rebuilding of Peterborough Abbey church was begun by Abbot Jean de Seez.

1194-97: the nave of the Abbey church was built and in 1238, the Abbey church (later to become Peterborough Cathedral) was consecrated.

1307: the first wooden bridge across the River Nene was constructed

1308: the diocese of Peterborough was formed out of Lincoln. Henry VIII established the former abbey church as Peterborough Cathedral, two years after the Dissolution.

1541: The Kings Grammar School for Boys was founded by Henry VIII as the Cathedral School, to educate the Cathedral choristers. This close link with the Cathedral is still valued and maintained today.

1574: the first of several outbreaks of a plague struck.

1586: Mary, Queen of Scots was imprisoned at Fotheringay Castle, near Peterborough.

1587: Mary Queen of Scots was buried in Peterborough Cathedral, after her execution at nearby Fotheringhay Castle. Her body was later moved to Westminster Abbey in 1612.

1617: the Market Cross, now the Guildhall, was built

End of 17th century: the population of the City stood at around 2,000.

1774: the first theatre was built.

1790: the Customs House was built.

1795: City's streets were lit with oil lamps for the first time.

The Guildhall in Cathedral Square, City Centre

1797: during the Napoleonic Wars, French prisoners of war were kept at a purpose-built camp at nearby Norman Cross until 1814.

1801: the population of the city was 4,075.

1830: gas street lighting was introduced in Peterborough.

1830: iron foundry opened.

1835: Poor Law Union was formed in December.

1847: the first railway line was introduced, from Blisworth in Northamptonshire to Peterborough. The station was opened by the London & Birmingham Railway.

1850: the Great Northern Railway opened the first main line from London to York through Peterborough.

1856: the Corn Exchange, in Church Street was built.

1856: St Peters Training College was built and in **1859,** the college was opened as a training college for schoolmasters.

1872: Peterborough Standard newspaper was launched.

1881: the population of the city according to the census was 19,846.

The Heritage of the Community

1891: the population increases to 25,171

1892: City's first public library opened.

1898: the Peterborough Citizen newspaper was launched.

1900: an electricity supply was introduced in the city.

1901: City population stood at around 30,872.

1903: electric trams were introduced in the city.

1910: Peterborough's first cinema was opened.

1911: City population was 33,574.

1921: City population increases to 35,532.

1930: the last electric trams in Peterborough were removed from service and replaced by buses.

1930-33: Peterborough Town Hall in Bridge Street was built.

Peterborough Museum, Priestgate

1931: the existing city Museum was opened

1931: the population of Peterborough was 43,551.

The Heritage of the Community

1932: Perkins Engines was established in Peterborough.

1934: Peterborough United Football Club was founded.

1934: a new bridge over the Nene was built.

1937: the Odeon Cinema was opened on Broadway.

1937: the Embassy Theatre was opened.

1939: the census counts the population as being 49,551.

1948: Peterborough Evening Telegraph newspaper was   launched.

1951: City population increases to 53,417.

1960: Peterborough United were elected to the Football League.

1961: population of city increases to 62,340.

1969: a new district hospital opened in Peterborough.

1971: City population was 69,556.

1973: the Key Theatre was built.

1978: the Nene Park was opened.

1981: population of city was 131,696.

1982: Queen Beatrix of the Netherlands opened Queensgate Shopping Centre.

1982: Flag Fen a Bronze Age archaeological site was discovered.

1982: the Peterborough Herald and Post newspaper was launched.

1991: the population of the city increases to 155,050.

2001: the population increases to 156,060.

2005: Her Majesty's Prison (HMP) was opened. It is one of the largest privately run category B prisons in the UK.

2011: the population of Peterborough city is estimated to be 164,000.

The city population is increasing, as the annual reported births are 3000 and deaths are 1500.

Queensgate Shopping Centre

Peterborough Town Hall, Bridge Street

Unitary Authority

In 1998, Peterborough city became autonomous of the Cambridgeshire County Council as a Unitary Authority, (but continues to form part of the county for ceremonial purposes). With the Unitary Authority status, the

City Council became responsible for providing all local government services previously provided by the Cambridgeshire County Council including Local Education Authority (LEA) maintained schools, socialservice functions from young peoples' welfare to elderly care, youth provisions, career advice and maintenance of roads. The Unitary Authority was linked with the new council structure for Councillors based on the Cabinet Model of decision-making similar to the National Government. This is where a council controlling party delegates cabinet positions to a few of its leading Councillors and in return, they are adequately rewarded with higher allowances for their increased responsibilities.

The New City Hospital in Peterborough

New City Hospital

In 2010, a new City hospital opened. The newly-built Peterborough City Hospital is a 611-bed hospital with a full range of specialties including a Cancer Centre, Cardiology Centre, a dedicated Women's and Children's Unit and Adult and Emergency Centre. Designed by Nightingale Associates, Peterborough City is the first new-build hospital in the UK to feature their innovative 'Cruciform' wards. Part of the £335 million Greater Peterborough Health Investment Plan, Peterborough City Hospital is the city's largest building project since the Cathedral was built in 1238. The new Peterborough City Hospital name was chosen by public competition in 2008.

Political Structure and Representation

The city has two Members of Parliament (MPs). Both are from the Conservative Party. North of the river Nene is represented by Stewart Jackson MP; whilst the South of Peterborough is represented by Shailesh Vara MP.

View of Bridge Street

A graph of city population since 1901

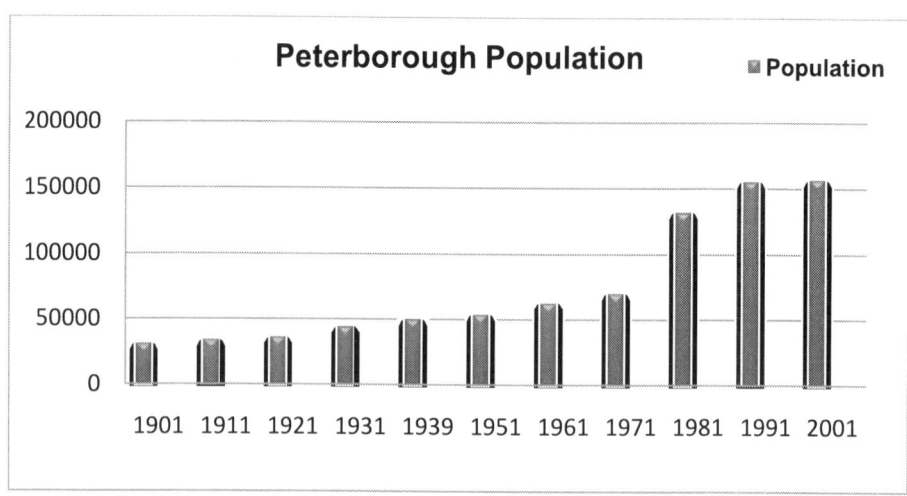

Peterborough and North West Cambridgeshire are included in the East of England Constituency for elections to the European Parliament and currently elects seven Members of the European Parliament (MEPs).

Peterborough City Council has 57 Ward Councillors and the Conservative Party is the current ruling party.

Friendship Links

At present Peterborough has twinning (friendship links) with five other European cities:

> - 1957 with Bourges, in central France, with a population of about 75,000.
> - 1982 with Viersen, in Germany, with a population of 75,000.
> - 1986 with Alcala de Henares, in central Spain, with a population of 204,000.
> - 1989 with Vinnitsa, located in the west of Ukraine (formerly part of the Soviet Union), with a population of 370,000.
> - 1991 with Forli, located in Italy, with a population of 117,000.

The city also has more informal friendship links with Foggia, Italy; Kwe Kwe, Zimbabwe; Pécs, Hungary; and all Peterboroughs around the world.

Main Employers

Peterborough has an established industry and to the present day, the industrial firms continue to create employment for a large working population. In the 2001 census, the city's workplace population was 90,476 divided into 60,118 people who live in Peterborough against 30,358 people who commute. The city's large employers are;

O Perkins Engines (now a subsidiary of Caterpillar Incorporation) has its UK head office in Peterborough. The firm established itself in the city in 1932. It primarily designs and manufactures diesel engines & gas turbines and other power generating equipment.
O Baker Perkins Ltd produces equipment and services for the food industry. Its Headquarters is based in Paston, Peterborough.
O Peter Brotherhood Ltd (acquired by Dresser-Rand in 2008) has its Peterborough base at Werrington Parkway. The firm provides

innovative engineering solutions for energy-related industries ranging from power generation to petrochemical processing.

O Peterborough City Council is responsible for providing local Unitary Authority services like Education, Social Services, Planning, Waste Disposal, Recycling and Collection, Trading Standards, Emergency Planning, Roads, Highways and Transportation, Housing, Environmental Health, Parks, Open Spaces and Countryside, plus Markets and Fairs and employs approximately 5,000 staff.

O The Regional Passport Office located at Northminster, Peterborough is one of only six offices in the country and employs about 600 people.

O The NHS' New City Hospital is also a large employer with 3,500 staff.

O Budget Insurance Services has its national head office in Bretton in Peterborough and currently employs 2,255 people.

Tourist Attractions

Peterborough has many tourist attractions in and around the city. Some of the main attractions include:

- Peterborough Cathedral is a 12th century building with the ruins of a medieval monastery, and is the burial place of Katharine of Aragon.
- Burghley House is an Elizabethan Stately home, located approximately 20 kilometres from Peterborough at Stamford.
- Nene Valley Railway, a heritage steam railway with working trains throughout the season from Peterborough to Wansford.
- The Museum and Art Gallery in Priestgate.
- Peterborough United Football Club at London Road.
- Queensgate and Rivergate Shopping Centres.
- Longthorpe Tower, a fortified 13th century house.
- Ferry Meadows Country Park and Orton Mere, west on the A605 road is a 500 acre site offering cycling, walking, kite-flying, pony riding, nature-spotting and fishing.
- Sacrewell Farm & Country Centre in Thornhaugh.
- St John the Baptist is Peterborough's Parish Church is an early 14th century church, located adjacent to St John's Square in City Centre.
- Flag Fen Bronze Age Site first discovered back in 1982 when a mechanical digger was working on one of the Fen drainage ditches at Northey Road Fengate in Peterborough. It provides an insight into life 3,000 years ago.
- East of England Country Show is held annually in June at the

The Heritage of the Community

Showground near Alwalton in Peterborough.

The Annual Peterborough Festival and Heritage Weekend held every June.

John Clare Cottage in Helpston is the home of this 19th century local poet.

Elton Hall is a 3,800-acre Estate house and gardens date back to the 15th century.

Prebendal Manor is 13th century house, including recreated medieval gardens and exhibitions at Nassington.

City Rankings

Peterborough is ranked 75th amongst the UK's most populated places.

In a recent survey for the UK's best towns and cities for drivers, Peterborough ranked eighth best in the UK.

Worldwide Peterboroughs

There are three other towns and a city named Peterborough around the world. They are all smaller in population than our UK city. The others are;

1. Peterborough of mid northern South Australia with a population of 1,683.
2. Peterborough in Victoria, Australia with a population of only 178.
3. Peterborough in Hillsborough County, New Hampshire, USA, with a population of 6,284.
4. Peterborough is a city on the Otonabee River in Southern Ontario, Canada, with a population of 74,888.

Peterborough Planned Expansion

As part of the Government's M11 corridor expansion, Peterborough is committed to creating 17,500 jobs with the population estimated to grow to 200,000 by 2020.

In the last 60 years immigration and asylum from different corners of the world is believed to have brought about half of the world's nationalities speaking about 100 different languages to our Cathedral city transforming it into a multi-cultural and very cosmopolitan city.

Peterborough Ethnic Groups

In June 2007, estimates by the Office for National Statistics give the following percentage breakdown of broad ethnic groups in Peterborough

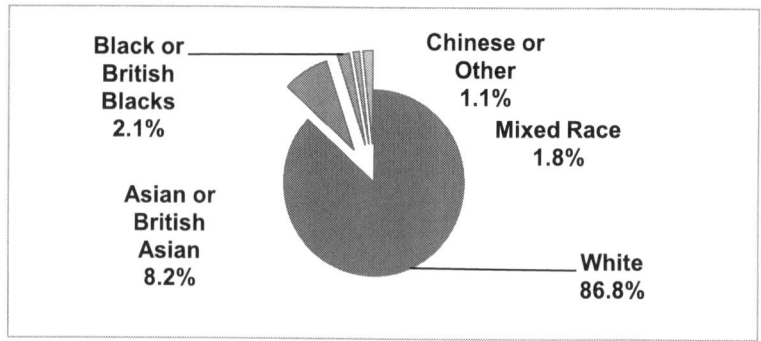

Peterborough Cathedral
The Heritage of the Community

Peterborough a Multicultural City

Background

Peterborough has always been a welcoming city for new immigrants and since the Second World War; there has been several visible changes in the immigrant populations.

Prior to the Second World War, the known small minority communities living in Peterborough were:

1. Roma
2. Jewish
3. Irish

These communities still have a presence in Peterborough. The Jewish community has a small Synagogue at 142 Cobden Avenue established in 1954.

Polish and Ukrainian

During the Second World War, a small number of Polish and Ukrainian men joined the Allied Forces and settled in the city after the war. They married local women and assimilated into mainstream society.

Italian Community

The Italians were the first immigrants to live and work in the city after

The Fleet Italian Community Centre

The Heritage of the Community

the Second World War and history records that the first connection between Peterborough and the Italians came during the Second World War when Italian prisoners of war were held in a POW camp at Norman Cross, on the outskirts of Peterborough. After the war, some released prisoners decided to remain in Peterborough and work for London Brick Company (LBC). In the 1950s, LBC carried out further labour recruitment in the Southern Italian regions of Puglia and Campania, which attracted a large number of Italian migrants to work in Peterborough specifically in the brickyards. By 1960, LBC employed approximately 3,000 Italian men, mostly at their Fletton works.

In the last 60 years, the Italian community has grown into one of the largest and well-established communities in the city. Peterborough has become home to one of the largest concentration of Italian immigrants in the UK. They are a hard working and proud community and with a strategy based on every man having a trade behind him, ranging from builder, carpenter, and plumber to electrician. A large number of Italians own and run catering bars and nightclubs, and local businesses. Most members of their community are living prosperous lives.

The present local Conservative Party Leader and the Peterborough City Council controlling party belongs to the British-Italian community. His name is Marco Cereste and he is a well known local figure. He was born Bovino in Foggia in Italy and migrated to Britain at a very young age. This was the time when many young families left southern Italy to work for the LBC in Peterborough.

The Italians have their own managed community centre called The Fleet in Fletton, Peterborough. The city areas with a large representation from the British-Italian community are: Fletton, Stanground and Woodston.

African Caribbean Community

In the 1950s, the new immigrants that followed the Italian community in Peterborough came from the Caribbean Islands. The African Caribbean immigrants were mostly from Jamaica, Trinidad and from other small English speaking West Indian islands. The men mainly worked on the railways and on the buses as conductors. Women worked for the National Health Service (NHS) as nurses and other support staff in hospitals. The Caribbean community was once very visible in the Gladstone Area. They had their own community centre called the Marcus Garvey Centre on Cromwell Road. The centre has since been demolished. In recent years, the community has integrated with the indigenous population through marriages or cohabiting partners and moved out of the area.

The Millennium African Caribbean Community Centre

The African Caribbean community does not have a large presence in any one specific Peterborough area. The Caribbean community have their own newly built community centre called the Millennium Centre off Dickens Street in the Eastfield Area.

Indian Community

In the late 1950s and early 1960s, small numbers of Indian nationals arrived in the city. They were Sikhs from the Punjab Province, who are also sometimes referred as Punjabi, soon after their arrival most went into corner shops and other small businesses. The early Punjabi community members also resided in the Gladstone Area. However, due to their growing prosperity, they quickly moved out into other middle-class city areas. Once the Sikh community had two- gurdwaras in the Gladstone Area in Cromwell Road and in Gladstone Street, but several years ago, both gurdwaras were vacated and have since sold the buildings to the members of the British-Pakistani community and they converted them into shops. The Sikh community has established two new gurdwaras on the outskirt of Fengate called Sri Guru Singh Sabha Gurdwara Sahib and Baba Budha Shaib Ji.

The Heritage of the Community

Bangladeshi Community

A handful of families belonging to the British-Bangladeshi community also live in Peterborough. They arrived in the city in the 1960s when their country was East Pakistan. The Bangladeshi community members have excellent understanding with the British-Pakistani community and use British-Pakistani community established built mosques and the local area Gladstone Park Community Centre.

East African Asian Community

For the next 10 years, there were no major immigration changes in Peterborough, apart from a small number of Asian refugees arriving in the city in 1972, when President Idi Amin Dada expelled them from Uganda. The expelled Ugandan refugees, along with the other small number of newly arrived immigrants from Kenya and Tanzania form part of the East African Asian Community.

The majority of East African Asians in Peterborough are Muslims and their roots are from the Indian state of Gujarat. They went to East African countries during the 19th century British colonial days, seeking employment and business opportunities and these countries formed a part of British Raj.

Hussaini Islamic Centre

The community is divided into three Muslim sects of Shia, Sunni and

Ismaili. Most members of the community are Shia Muslims and residents of Eastgate and the Eastfield Areas. Their community first established an Imam Bargah and Hussaini Islamic Centre in 1975 at Burton Street.

In 1992, to accommodate the increasing population the community had their own purpose built Hussaini Islamic Centre. This was the first purpose built Islamic Centre in the region with a capacity of 550 people including provision for women.

The Sunni members of the East African community are the second largest and they have a considerable presence in Orton Goldhay and in Orton Malborne. They worship in British-Pakistani community established mosques and use the Gladstone Park Community Centre.

The third smaller sect is the Ismaili Muslim community is known by two identities;

- Shia Imma Nizari Ismaili
- Dawoodi Bohra Muslim Association

The Shia Ismali community is larger of the two communities and their Jamat Khunna was established in the 1980s at Craig Street. The community is scattered throughout the city and their congregations include people of East African Asians, Indian and Pakistani origins.

The Dawoodi Bohra Community members are the former residents of Uganda. They established a community association hall in Craig Street in 1999 converting from a builder's yard. The Dawoodi Bohra Community members mainly manage their own businesses and consist of just closely related families numbering about 45/50 people living in and around the city.

There are a number of Gujarati East African Asians belonging to the Hindu community in Peterborough. They are small in population and scattered all over the city. They have their own community centre with a temple called Bharat Hindu Samaj, which is in the New England Complex Centre.

At one time most of Peterborough's immigrants were either from Italy or from the former British Colony countries that now form part of the New Commonwealth.

North African Students

In the 1980s, Peterborough witnessed the arrival of students from North Africa, from Libya and Morocco. They studied at the Peterborough Regional College. The majority returned to their home countries after completing their studies with a small minority remaining in Peterborough.

Refugees and Asylum Seekers

The next big change was the arrival of people seeking refuge and asylum in the UK under the Geneva Convention of 1951. They came from all over the world in the 1990s. Peterborough had its fair share of the new arrivals. They arrived from both the Turkish and Iraqi Kurdish regions, Afghanistan, Somalia, Democratic Republic of Congo (formerly known as Zaire), Rwanda, Zimbabwe, Bosnia, Kosovo, East Timor and a number of Eastern European countries. With the exception of the Eastern Europeans, all the other nationalities of refuge/asylum seekers were young men. The greatest numbers came from Afghanistan and the Kurdish region of Northern Iraq.

Eastern and Southern Europeans

In May 2004, Slovakia, Czech Republic, Poland, Hungary, Slovenia, Estonia, Latvia and Lithuania joined the European Union (EU), which gave their citizens rights to live in and work in any EU country. This came with the requirement that they must register for work when they arrive and forfeit any work-related state benefits until they have been in paid work for a year. Children are entitled to benefits, so any EU parent citizens could claim Child Benefit. Soon after these countries joined the EU, Peterborough's immigrant community population increased by many fold after the arrival of tens of thousands of new immigrants, described as the free movement of people within the EU countries of Eastern and Southern Europe. These people are from Poland, Czech Republic, Slovakia, Portugal (already an EU member since 1986) and from the Baltic States of Latvia, Lithuania and Estonia. The two of the largest new arrivals in Peterborough are the Polish and Portuguese communities. Both communities are very different from each other especially in their work etiquettes. The Polish people are working all available hours whilst the Portuguese people appear to live a relaxed Southern European life.

It is reported that about 120 million people worldwide do not live in their birth country.

Main Attractions

Employment opportunities and the availability of social and private sector housing are major attractions for new immigrants. Peterborough has traditionally low levels of unemployment which makes it an attractive destination for migrant workers. As well as the large established city employers there are many farming related jobs from picking fruit to packing vegetables in small farm factories on the outskirts of the city and in the neighbouring districts, although these jobs are often seasonal, poorly paid and hard to fill from the local population.

The Gladstone Area

Historically, all new immigrants arriving in Peterborough first settled in the Gladstone Area of the city. After the Second World War, the first migrant community to have lived in the area were the Italians and they were followed by the Caribbean migrants and later by the Pakistani migrant community. The Gladstone Area is an inner city area located within walking distance from the city centre as well as other amenities like the railway and the bus stations. The Gladstone area's housing stock is old and densely populated. The newly arrived migrants found a comfort zone with other migrants making the area an ideal choice for new arrivals. Migrants use the Gladstone Area as the transit point before dispersing to other parts of the city. The recent mass arrival in Peterborough from the EU countries has greatly regenerated the Gladstone Area and this has largely benefitted the area established British-Pakistani community. The local shopkeepers and other businesses operating in the area were struggling to survive but with the arrival of the new communities, they have dramatically increased their businesses ensuring profit and sustainability.

Multiculturalism

Today, people of all nationalities, ethnic backgrounds, and religious beliefs (estimated to be about 14 different faiths) are living side-by-side generally in peace, tolerance and harmony in Peterborough. It is widely recognised that the five largest black and minority ethnic communities now residing in Peterborough are the two embedded communities namely: British-Italian and British-Pakistani. The three newly arrived communities include Lithuanian, Polish and Portuguese.

British-Pakistani Community in Peterborough

Background

The first Pakistani community connection with Peterborough was a conflicting topic amongst the elder surviving members of this community. After meeting many earliest arrivals to the city, it was not clear which member of the community arrived first in the city. I made a conscious decision to research the subject for definitive evidence before attempting to name the first person.

Research

I felt that the best way forward would be to carry out research by inspecting the Electoral Registers and I spent a considerable amount of time inspecting the Peterborough Electoral Registers from 1950 to 1960/61. The very first community member's names, which appeared on the Register was in 1959/60 and they were Noogrn Mohammad and Kluzir Mohammad at 110 Russell Street. The closing deadline for the registration was 10th October 1958. The following year 1960/61, the Electoral Registration from the same address was under the name of Mohammed Suleman and the closing registration deadline was on 10th October 1959.

According to Haji Mohammed Suleman, now one of the surviving elder members of the community, he purchased the house from Chaudhry Fakeer Mohammed and that he along with his indigenous wife were residents in the property. After evaluating the situation, it makes sense that Chaudhry Fakeer Mohammed's passport name was Noogrn Mohammed and his wife was called Kluzir Mohammed. Although I am aware, most early arrivals were illiterate or probably unsure about the Electoral Registration process but my evidence is based on recorded information.

First Arrival

After considering the evidence, I am happy to confirm Noogrn Mohammed alias Chaudhry Fakeer Mohammed from the Kotli district in Azad Jammu and Kashmir was indeed the first Pakistani to have arrived in Peterborough.

Late Chaudhry Fakeer Mohammed, the first Pakistani to have arrived in Peterborough

I have further identified some of the known earliest arrivals in the city and they were:

1. Late Chaudhry Rahmat Khan of village of Orangabad from Sarai Alamgir
2. Late Chaudhry Muhammed Sarwar from Charhi
3. Late Mohammed Fazil of Kerri from Islamgarh
4. Late Karamat Hussain of Kalyal Bainsi from Islamgarh
5. Late Khadam Hussain of Potha Bainsi
6. Haji Mohammed Suleman of Kaneli
7. Ali Haider of Check Hariam

Another elder member of the community is Mohammed Nazir from the village Kalyal Bainsi. According to him he arrived in Peterborough in May 1958 with two other friends Fazal Hussain and Mohammed Yaqoob. A mutual friend provided them with transport from Bedford and informed them that Peterborough was a city of opportunity with good employment prospects. Unfortunately, the three had only been in the country for a short period and were unfamiliar as to how to acquire living accommodation and at nightfall without much choice, the three spent their first night in the town centre under at the historic Guildhall building. Their second night was spent in the railway station waiting room. On the third day, in sheer desperation, they headed towards the nearest residential area, Cromwell Road and knocked on residents doors and asked for accommodation. All three were lucky to find accommodation on an individual basis with Italian families.

My late father Haji Anayat Ali from the village Morah Bari in Islamgarh was also amongst the early arrivals in the city in 1959. Father first arrived in Sheffield in 1958, and a few months later moved to Nottingham in search of employment and several months later came to Peterborough. My father was employed by the London Brick Yard as a truck driver and he lodged with an Italian family in Stanground.

Employment Prospects

According to the earliest arrivals, Peterborough was renowned for its good employment prospects in the brickyard industry, and Perkins Engines was actively recruiting workers. In addition, several smaller foundries such as Die Casting and Combex Limited were seeking workers. After the first migrant arrived in the city, many other members of the community followed through their connections. This enabled the city's community to grow and establish a permanent base in Peterborough.

Employment

The newly arrived migrants were often employed on unskilled, low paid, noisy and demanding jobs. Many worked on permanent night shift jobs and that was because the local indigenous people declined to accept these jobs citing them as being undesirable. Migrants worked from 12 -16 hours a day and earned £5-£6 a week. Most walked several kilometres (sometimes even up to 15 kilometres) to and from work on a daily bias. This took considerable time but they were a determined, resilient and high spirited group of people and nothing seemed impossible to them. The newly arrived men were young fit and healthy seeking paid employment and were taking jobs at brick yards, small foundries or the railways.

Restricted Diet

The early migrants faced a restrictive diet as no halal meat or spices were available locally. The community was dependent on live poultry sold at the Cattle Market or they travelled to the nearest cities of Nottingham or Leicester to buy their essentials. In the early 1960s, Chaudhry Mohammed Aurangzeb opened a halal butchery & grocery shop on Cromwell Road. This provided the community with the dietary requirements it needed.

Whilst discussing the community dietary needs, I am reminded of a well-known Englishman by the name of Bill who sold live poultry, fresh fruit and vegetables door-to-door to the British-Pakistan community in the Gladstone Area, in a small truck with his son. He must have traded with the community for 30 to 40 years.

Gladstone Area History

After the Pakistani migrants' arrival in the city, they quickly established a base in the Gladstone Area. Their main reason for selecting this area was largely affordable housing the community continued with the Pakistani traditional trend of owning their houses, which they have a great deal of pride and call as their own. Even today that trend continues very few British-Pakistani members of the community renting either privately or live in a social housing accommodation. The area was within walking distance of other essential amenities like the railway and the bus station. Today the Gladstone Area is considered one of the most deprived and the poorest areas in the whole country. History state that the area's land was owned by the Church of England. Around 1860 the church decided to sell the land for residential development and local residents purchased plots of land and constructed their own developments. One of the visible signs of this is the external stone plaques on the houses with names like Edward or Smith terraces with the construction dates.

Early Racism

Apart from culinary complications, another major problem early migrants had was with direct rampant racism, where people were racially abused, intimidated, threatened, chased whilst walking alone, physically attacked and so called "Paki bashing" was a regular occurrence. The earliest generations were very law-abiding, non-confrontational people and they generally accepted that racism was part of their everyday life to be endured. Sadly, racism has claimed several young people lives in Peterborough.

Despite enduring daily racism, many members of the community have positive memories about their early days while seeking help from the likes of taxi drivers and police officers to search for and to reach their destinations' as most spoke very little English and usually had a piece of paper with an address written on it.

The Gladstone Mural

Establishing Mosques

In the mid 1960s, the community had considerably grown in population and after hiring venues for Friday and Eid prayers, some leading community activists include:

> Late Chaudhry Mohammed Aurangzeb
> Haji Bagh Ali
> Late Chaudhry Muhammed Sarwar
> Late Haji Fazal Karim
> Late Haji Muzaffar Hussain
> Late Babu Mohammed Azam
> Late Babu Fazal Hussain
> Late Raja Rashid Ahmed
> Babu Mohammed Hussain
> Late Mohammed Riaz
> Haji Sheikh Mohammed Rafique
> Late Haji Karamat Hussain (President)

The most instrumental person in the community was the late Chaudhry Mohammed Aurangzeb who headed the campaign to establish a mosque. In consultation with the community, they purchased a detached building in Cromwell Road for £2,800 and with Local Authority; consent converted the building into a mosque. To finance the building, every employed member of the British-Pakistani community was asked to donate one-week's wages toward the mosque funds and all members of the community happily followed the appeal instruction.

In 1967, the first Peterborough city mosque was established at 60 Cromwell Road and it served the religious needs of all citywide Muslims.

First Mosque in Peterborough at 60 Cromwell Road

The overwhelming population of the British-Pakistani community members are Sunni Muslims and 60 Cromwell Road was the Sunnat al Jamat mosque.

The mosque committee made provisions for after-school Religious Education classes for all community young boys. Prior to the establishment of the mosque at 60 Cromwell Road, the late Chaudhry Mohammed Aurangzeb voluntarily allocated a section of his shop to enable the community to facilitate Religious Education classes for young boys.

Ghousia Mosque

Some 14 years later, the community had further grown in population and became scattered throughout the Gladstone Area. A number of vocal community activists felt that the walking distance from the upper end of Gladstone Street to the Cromwell Road mosque was too far for young boys to walk in the cold and dark winter months. A consultation and fund raising campaign was led by the late Chaudhry Arshad Ahmed and members of the community residing in upper Gladstone Area approved the proposal to support the fund raising to establish a second mosque in the Gladstone Area.

In 1981 after raising sufficient funds, they purchased a detached house at 405 Gladstone Street for £24,000 and with Local Authority; approval converted the building into the new Ghousia mosque. The new mosque fulfilled the community religious requirements and made provisions for after school hours Religious Education for young boys.

UK Islamic Mission

In 1986 a group of community members decided to set up a UK Islamic Mission (UKIM) branch in Peterborough with combined mosque facilities. They purchased a detached house on 311 Cromwell Road for £10,000 and with approval of the Local Authority converted the building into the Masjid Khadijah and Islamic Centre. The person who facilitated the campaign and played an active role by fund raising was the late Hafiz Abdul Malik. Some 20 years later, to meet the expending community needs the mission also purchased an adjacent property for £60,000.

Dar Assalaam Mosque

In 1997, a small group of community members purchased a former hotel building at 80-82 Alma Road for £110,000 and with the Local Authority approval led the building conversion into the Dar Assalaam mosque.

Socio-Economic Factors

In a similar pattern to other British towns and cities, Peterborough has both working and middle-class members within the community. Statistically, the British-Pakistani community is one of the most disadvantaged communities in Britain and is more likely to be considered poor under official classifications than the indigenous community. However, macro-analyses and population averages hide considerable regional, class and ethnic variations. Despite being below average on most socio-economic indicators, the British-Pakistani population is steadily improving and the community is striving to work hard and commit long hours, with aspirations to improving their quality of lives. It is evident that their efforts have paid off with dividends.

Purpose Built Mosques

In the 2001 UK National Census, the British-Pakistani community population in Peterborough was 6,000. 10 years later, it is now estimated that the current British-Pakistani population is around 10,000. The majority of these have their roots in the Mirpur district of Azad Jammu and Kashmir. In the last 10 years, the community has further established itself by becoming strong, stable, embedded and prosperous.

The Jamia and Ghousia mosque committee members made a conscious decision in their respective management committee meetings that their mosques converted from houses had served their purpose. Thus, in order to meet the growing community requirements the only way forward was to build purpose built mosques with greater capacities and with modern day essentials such as car parking.

"The heritage of the community gives recognition to both mosque committee members for being forward thinkers, showing leadership qualities, being creative, visionary and by undertaking momentous decisions to proceed with purpose built mosques."

The Jamia Mosque committee had wisely purchased an old sizeable factory with ample land on the junction between the Link Road and Gladstone Street several years earlier with a view for a for new mosque building at the price of £160,000.

The Ghousia Mosque committee had also purchased an adjacent garage and car parking land for £45,000 from the City Council in the mid 1990s. I was also involved in negotiation meetings between the Ghousia Mosque Committee and the City Council Senior Officers.

The Jamia Mosque committee went through an extensive wave of consultations with the community to ascertain their views on the new proposed Faizan-e-Madinah Mosque and on the issue of fundraising for the mosque. The man who headed the campaign initiative was the late Chaudhry Maqbool Hussain, the Chairman of the mosque committee. The community unanimously endorsed the new mosque proposal with a commitment and immediately started their donations for the new mosque project. The mosque committee initially collected £250 from every registered member towards the new mosque project. Later a further £1,000 was collected from every registered member. Women members of the community played an important role by donating a significant amount of their gold jewellery towards the mosque funds. Once the committee felt satisfied that a sufficient amount of funds had been raised they proceeded with the work.

Faizan-e-Madinah Mosque

Work commenced in December 2001 on the new Faizan-e-Madinah Mosque at 169-175 Gladstone Street and Hazrat Sahibzada Pir Mohammad Habib-ur-Rahman Mahboobi laid the foundation stone.

"Sadly, soon after laying the mosque foundation the man with the grand vision and aspiration to complete the multimillion-pound mosque project, Chaudhry Maqbool Hussain, died suddenly. His untimely death created a huge impact on the project and left an enormous vacuum in the community".

During the construction of the new mosque building, the committee encountered some difficulties with contractors, resulting in several years delay and the work was finally completed in 2006. The total mosque building costs were £3 million. Marble and other construction material was imported from Pakistan. The estimated mosque capacity is 3,000 people. Thanks to the mosque committee members for their forward thinking and wisely putting aside a considerable amount of their funds for many years the new mosque was able to be built. Our Peterborough British-Pakistani community is probably the only unique Muslim community in the whole of the UK to have raised £3 million entirely from the donations by the local British-Pakistani community.

Ghousia Mosque

Soon after the Faizan-e-Madinah Mosque foundation, work also commenced on this second purpose built new Ghousia Mosque at 406 Gladstone Street with large waves of donations from within the local community. Once again, women from the community played a prominent role by donating considerable amounts of their gold jewellery. The committee set a 12-month work completion target date. Work commenced on the new £1.4 million mosque in 2002 and was completed in 2004. The estimated mosque capacity is 1,200 people. Here again, the local Peterborough British-Pakistani community met all building costs from subscriptions and the generous donations within the community.

I congratulate both the Jamia Mosque and Ghousia committee members for their achievements in building such an excellent grand mosques to serve the present and future Muslim community needs in Peterborough.

Faizan-e-Madinah Mosque Committee

The new Faizan-e-Madinah Mosque committee is responsible for the management of the mosque. The committee's priorities are to have anopen door policy by welcoming enquiries and visits to the mosque. In 2010, over 2,000 schoolchildren visited the mosque. The committee operates a new Muslim initiative and works in partnership with other Peterborough based religious organisations and multi-agencies. The committee encourages Imams to attend training courses including chaplaincy and English courses to ensure effective communication with all sections of the community, especially young people, as well as acquiring new and updated skills.

Faizan-e-Madinah Mosque in Peterborough

Ghousia Mosque Committee

The new Ghousia Mosque Committee is responsible for the day-to-day management of the mosque. The committee's priorities are to maximise ongoing educational and religious knowledge visits for non-Muslim young people, raise funds for various worldwide emergency disasters including the Turkish and Chinese earthquakes, the 2005 Boxing Day Tsunami and the more recent Pakistani earthquake. The committee raised and donated £26,000 to build 30 essential wooden dwellings in the Neelum valley in Kashmir and the work has since been completed. The committee also encourages Religious Education Teachers to attend relevant training in response to contemporary issues and support Imams in attending English classes. At present, around 300 young children are attending Religious Education classes held at the mosque.

Ghousia Mosque in Peterborough

Since the opening of both the Faizan-e-Madinah and new Jamia Ghousia Mosques, respective committee members have invited world eminent Muslim scholars to spread the teaching of Islam amongst the young people and in the Peterborough British-Pakistani community.

Masjid Khadijah & Islamic Centre

The refurbishment of the Masjid Khadijah & Islamic Centre at 311 – 313 Cromwell Road began in 2008 and was completed in 2010 at a cost of around £250,000. The new masjid has the capacity for 450 people, living quarters for two Imams with a kitchen, library, IT facilities and a youth centre. Masjid Khadijah & Islamic Centre is a part of the national UKIM organisation and both males and females are members of the management committee. The masjid is open for everyone and the congregation is made up of all nationalities.

UKIM Masjid Khadijah & Islamic Centre

Dar Assalaam Mosque (under construction)

Dar Assalaam Mosque

Since 2009, work has been progressing well on the new 500 people capacity mosque. The building work is being carried out in three phases with the completion phase scheduled at the end of 2011 at a total estimated cost of £1 million.

Madrassas

There are several madrassas (religious schools) throughout Peterborough. The madrassas operate independently from the city's mosques and are privately owned and registered with the Local Authority and some are registered under the Charities Commission. Peterborough's operational madrassas are:

- Madrassa Qassmia Taleem-ul-Quran at 4 Bamber Street
- Jamia Madina Tul Islam operates at 98a Dogsthorpe Road
- Al-Mustafa Quran Academy at 33 Parliament Street
- Jamia Fazal-ul-Aloom is based at 182 St Pauls Road

Community Population

For the last half century, the Gladstone Area has been the established base of the British-Pakistani community in Peterborough, although large numbers of the community members also reside in other areas of the city namely: New England, West Town, Park Ward, Dogsthorpe and Eastgate

In recent years, the community population has outgrown what the Gladstone Area can provide. This is resulting in even greater numbers of residents requiring relocating to more affluent areas of the city such as Park Ward, Netherton and Longthorpe.

Self Employed

A high percentage of the British-Pakistani community members are self-employed, working as taxi drivers, Indian restaurants and in fast-food outlets. They often work long and unsociable hours to provide first-rate community services. Without these two essential services (transport and food), I am certain that life would be very different for residents and visitors to Peterborough.

Community Prosperity

Since the closure of many old established heavy industries, (remember the British saying risks create opportunities) new sets of opportunities have been created in other sectors for the entrepreneurial members of the British-Pakistani community. Their new established businesses are in second-hand car dealers/garages, property letting management services, insurance companies, supplying workforce, 'buy-to-let' properties and property trading as well as managing other successful businesses. Many have become prosperous through their new businesses and this has become evident in their improved life styles buying expensive cars; their children being educated at private schools; taking more foreign holidays; and residing in more prestigious 'upmarket' areas of Peterborough.

Links with Pakistan

British-Pakistani families have maintained close links with Pakistan ever since their arrival in the UK. Travel between Pakistan and the UK has been a strong link. People often send remittances to their families back home. This is a critical element of keeping in touch and providing for their families back in Pakistan. Whilst the tradition is still maintained, it is not at the same level as the days of early migration. British-Pakistanis remain highly engaged with politics as it unfolds in Pakistan and there are many formal visits by politicians on both sides. Another key influence that drives political links is the effort by Pakistani political parties to establish their political structures and affiliations within the UK. These parties have local office bearers in Britain, which creates a local medium for political, social and religious links, both for individuals and groups, as well as fundraising within the UK. There are substantial business and commercial links between Pakistan and the UK. Additionally, the existences of various national charitable organisations that work in Pakistan and Azad Jammu and Kashmir have assisted in maintaining these close links.

Friendship Links with Mirpur City

In 2004/05, while Raja Akhtar Hussain Raja was the Mayor of Peterborough, constructive efforts were made to establish links between Peterborough and the city of Mirpur in Azad Jammu and Kashmir. Correspondence was exchanged with the Mirpur Municipal Corporation with the intent to establishing friendship links between the two cities. Peterborough City Council Directors Group requested a presentation with an explanation on how both cities could benefit by forging such links and the areas in which Peterborough City Council could assist Mirpur Municipal Corporation and the citizens of Mirpur city. Ansar Ali and Raja Tahir Masood made a PowerPoint presentation in attendance of Chief Executive. The presentation was well received and appreciated. Peterborough City Council formed a Mirpur Friendship Links Committee. However, regrettably the friendship proposal did not progress further due to a lack of communication from the Mirpur Municipal Corporation. The outcome was clearly disappointing after considerable time and effort had gone into the project via the City Council Link Committee, Mayor and the two presenters.

Iqra Girls Academy

One of the recent successful projects founded by the British-Pakistani community in Peterborough is the Iqra Girls Academy established in 2009 by the Peterborough Muslim Education Trust (PMET). This is a voluntary and charitable organisation established with the primary aim of meeting the educational needs of the Muslim community.

The Iqra Girls Academy opened in September 2009 to Year 7 & 8 students. The Academy is a private institution and runs without any Local Authority or Central Government grants. Admissions are open to all members and the Academy is a fee-charging establishment.

Current Forms of Racism

Although today, most British-Pakistani community members are British by birth they do not openly tolerate abuse or racism and will challenge racists in reality, they are still experiencing racism and prejudice these include:

1 Race hate crime
2 Indirect racism

Race hate crimes have nevertheless been on the rise with a number of victims lodging complaints so that recorded crime is now on the increase. These crimes range from Swastikas being smeared on buildings to verbal and physical attacks. The number of crimes tagged with a "hate crime marker" (where a victim believes an incident has undertones of racism).

Indirect forms of racism, or 'hidden racism' as it is some time described, is where people suffer daily discrimination at their work place. This includes disproportionate competition for employment, training, pay and promotion.

Patriotism

Recently, I met a young British-Pakistani man and the first thing I noticed about him was a visible tattoo of a 'crescent and star' on his neck. While holding a conversation with him I asked him about his tattoo and he responded by saying that although he considered himself British, he is also proud of his Pakistani heritage and the 'crescent and star' is his way of expressing and making a statement about his Pakistani origins.

Minority Ethnic Communities

The British-Pakistani community live in peace and harmony with the other local minority ethnic communities residing in Peterborough. However, one minority community stands out from the rest and that is the British-Italian community. The British-Italian community stood 'shoulder to shoulder' with the British-Pakistani community. Both of these established minority communities displayed a mutual respect and work collaboratively to present unity regardless of their political parties. The three other large new communities in Peterborough are the Polish, Portuguese and Lithuanians and they are still in the process of establishing in the city.

The arrival of immigrants after the Second World War from all over the world has made the UK one of the largest multi-cultural societies in the world.

British-Pakistani and Muslim Community in the United Kingdom

Background

The major cause of migration from Pakistan to the UK was economic; many people were in search of better opportunities to support themselves and their families. The earliest migrants mostly filled the unskilled labour gaps and took poorly paid jobs, which were available because of the reconstruction and expansion of the UK economy post 1945.

British-Pakistani Population

It is estimated that currently 1.2 million people of British-Pakistani origin are now living in the UK, making them the largest overseas Pakistani population anywhere in the world. This is even larger than the Pakistani community in Saudi Arabia, which is estimated to be around 1.1 million.

Community Prominence

After half a century of British-Pakistani community presence in the UK, the community plays a prominent role in everyday life, from Doctors to MPs from self-employed taxi drivers to owners of large cash and carry businesses. There are far more self-employed members of the British-Pakistani than any other minority group.

Famous Figures

I have included a list of some well-known British-Pakistani figures in the UK:

- **Amir Iqbal Khan,** the current boxing WBA World Light Welterweight Champion and the Olympic silver medallist for the Team Great Britain.

- **Sajjad Haider Karim** is a Member of the European Parliament (MEP) for North West England. Karim was the first British Muslim elected to the European Parliament.

- **James Caan** (formerly Nazim Khan) is a British-Pakistani investor, entrepreneur and television personality. Caan known for his appearance as the member of the investor panel on BBC's Dragons' Den series.

- **Lord Nazir Ahmed** is a member of the House of Lords and only the second Muslim life peer.

- **Sir Anwar Pervez** is a Pakistani-born businessman and one of the richest Asians in Great Britain. He is the founder of the Bestway Group and a self-made owner of companies worth billions of pounds.

- **Baroness Sayeeda Warsi** is the current Co-Chairman of the Conservative Party that is part of the present coalition government, alongside the Liberal Democrats.

It is impossible to mention all the members of the community who have achieved success. However, it is estimated that more than 100 British-Pakistanis are multi-millionaires. One recent survey found 34% of British-Pakistanis classified themselves as being 'middle class' whilst the majority considered themselves to be working class.

The British-Pakistani Community

The majority of British-Pakistani community members are born in the UK, almost all others have British nationalities, and therefore it is inconsistent for the community to be called 'immigrants' or 'foreigners they are simply British-Pakistanis. Despite varying experiences of racism, poverty and other social inequalities, the British-Pakistani community feels and truly believes it has strong and indispensable connections with Britain.

Poverty Line

In 2007, the findings of Joseph Rowntree foundation were that British-Pakistanis have the second highest 'relative poverty' rates in Britain, as 55% live in poverty, and are ranked just behind the Bangladeshis. This is in comparison to only 20% of the indigenous people living in poverty. The poverty line is classified as the minimum level of income threshold that is necessary to achieve an adequate living standard in the UK.

Community Information

- ♯ In 2005, it was recorded that at least 3.7% of children born in England and Wales had two British-Pakistani origin parents.
- ♯ The other national statistics about the community are that British-Pakistani pupils are the largest ethnic minority group in both primary and secondary schools in the UK.
- ♯ A recent BBC report found that 55% of British-Pakistanis are marrying their first cousins.

The following are population figures of British-Pakistanis in the UK.

Year	Population
2001	750,000
1991	480,000
1981	300,000
1971	120,000
1961	25,000
1951	10,000

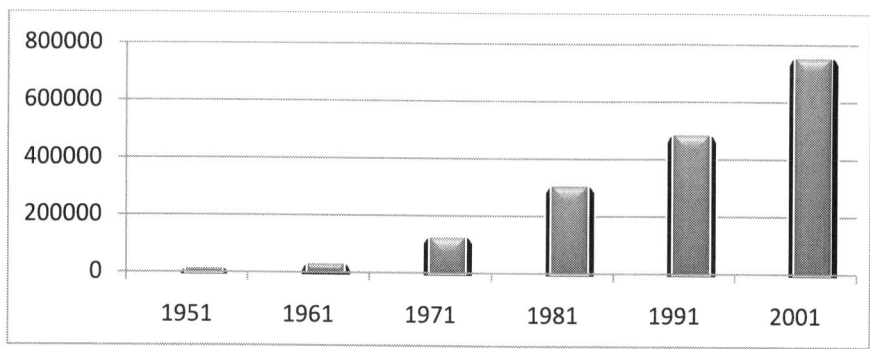

The following are community population figures, although these are several years old but the only available figures on the British-Pakistani community in the UK. The area based community population figures were in 2005 apart from the London and its figures are from 2007.

- ¤ The estimated population of British-Pakistanis living in London was 179,000. They represent the most diverse community made up of Mirpuris, Punjabis, Pathans, Balochis, Urdu speaking Muhajirs and Sindhis. Their largest presence is in the East London areas of Ilford, Walthamstow, Leyton, Barking and Newham.
- ¤ The West Midlands is home to 172,000 people of British-Pakistani community origin. Birmingham has 113,000 British-Pakistanis making up 11.2% of the city's population and is one of the largest Pakistani expatriate communities in the world. The largest concentrations are in Birmingham's inner city and areas such as Alum Rock and Balsall Heath.
- ¤ 163,000 British-Pakistanis live in Yorkshire - with Bradford being home to an estimated 80,000 who make up 16.1% of the city's population.
- ¤ 133,000 British-Pakistanis live in the North West of England.

The large towns and cities with estimated British-Pakistani community populations in 2007 and percentages of local population:

- o Kirklees   28,600 (7.1)
- o Manchester   28,100 (6.1)
- o Newham   23,000 (9.2)
- o Luton   20,100 (10.6)
- o Waltham Forest   17,500 (7.8)
- o Leeds   18,200 (2.4)
- o Redbridge   17,800 (7.0)
- o Sheffield   17,400 (3.3)
- o Rochdale   17,200 (8.4)
- o Oldham   15,300 (7.0)
- o Slough   14,600 (12.2)
- o Blackburn   12,900 (9.0)
- o Ealing   12,400 (4.0)
- o Hounslow   10,200 (2.8)

Today, members of the British-Pakistani community live in every British town and city and the greatest numbers are located in:

Aylesbury, Birmingham, Blackburn, Bedford, Bolton, Bradford, Bristol, Burnley, Burton-on-Trent, Bury, Cardiff, Coventry, Derby, Dudley, Dundee, Glasgow, Edinburgh, Halifax, Huddersfield, Leeds, Leicester, London, Luton, Manchester, Middlesbrough, Nelson, Nottingham, Newcastle-Upon-Tyne, Oldham, Oxford, Peterborough, Preston, Reading, Rochdale, Rotherham, Rugby, Sheffield, Slough, Stockport, Stoke-on-Trent, Walsall, Watford, Wolverhampton and Worcester.

As already stated, the British-Pakistani community is the largest Muslim group in the UK. According to the 2001 Census, 98% of the British-Pakistani community living in the UK are Muslim with 2% from other religions including the 1% Christian community now estimated to be about 10,000 British-Pakistani Christians residing in the UK making it one of the largest overseas British-Pakistani Christian communities. It is estimated that by 2031 the population of the British-Pakistani community in the UK will increase to 2.63 million from the current estimate of 1.2 million.

British-Pakistani Community

In Britain, the British-Pakistanis are now living in all geographic areas and because of their dedication to hard work many have became very prosperous and highly successful. Mirpur is one of the principal sources of migration from Pakistan to Europe, especially to Britain in the last five decades and it is now estimated that about 60–70% of the British-Pakistani community is of Mirpuri descent, which is more than the present population of the Mirpur district. The Mirpur district population is approximately 370,000 people, with Mirpur city population standing at around 100,000 people.

Muslim Population in UK

The current Muslim population in Britain is about 3 million, which is equivalent to 4.6% of the population and it is estimated that the Muslim population in the UK will almost double to 5.5% within 20 years. The Muslim communities have established about 1500 mosques. The Muslim birth rate is roughly three times higher than the non-Muslim rate. Furthermore, it is estimated that the last year 5,200 British people converted to Islam and it is now believed that about 100,000 which includes indigenous and other British citizens have embraced Islam. The average age of newly convert profile is about 27, white and female.

While discussing Islam in Britain I recently discovered that the earliest known Englishman to embrace Islam happened in the 16th century. His name was John Nelson and the 16th century writer Richard Hakluyt mentioned him in his book 'Voyager's Tales'.

Muslim Population in UK

Year	Population
2011	2,800,000
2008	2,422,000
2007	2,327,000
2006	2,142,000
2005	2,017,000
2004	1,870,000
1990	1,100,000

Mohammed is most popular name

Mohammed is now the most popular name for newborn boys in the UK. The official list covers all births in 2010 in England and Wales and Mohammed comes in at number 9. However, this does not include the many different spellings ranked separately. When added in total, Mohammed zooms all the way up to the top spot for the first time. Last year 7,549 newborns babies were given 14 variations of Mohammed's name. In order of popularity the variant spellings used during the year were:

Muhammad, Mohammad, Muhammed, Mohamed, Mohamad, Muhamed, Mohammod, Mahamed, Muhamad, Mahammed, Mohmmed. Muhammod, Mohamud and Mohammud.

There are other possible spellings but these were not used for births in England and Wales. Regionally, the single spelling of Mohammed comes top.

Mohammed Listing

Year	Listing order
2010	9
2009	16
2008	16
2007	17
2006	22

European Countries Muslim Populations

The UK has the third largest Muslim community on the European continent after:

Germany	4,019,000	5%
France	3,574,000	5.7%:
Belgium		6%
Austria and Switzerland		5.7%
Netherlands		5.5%
Sweden		4.9%
Greece		4.7%

Expatriate Community Populations

Seven million Pakistanis are living outside Pakistan, which is about 4% of the country's population. Countries with Pakistani populations are:

Country	Population
United Kingdom	1,200,000
Saudi Arabia	1,100,000
United Arab Emirates	1,100,000
United States	700,000
Canada	300,000
Kuwait	100,000
Italy	100,000
Oman	85,000
Greece	80,000
France	60,000
Qatar	52,000
Spain	47,000
Bahrain	45,500
Netherlands	40,000
Germany	35,000
Denmark	21,000
Norway	30,000
Libya	30,000
Australia	20,000
Hong Kong	20,000
Belgium	14,500
Ireland	12,500
Japan	12,000
Iran	11,500
Turkey	10,000

Educational Progressions

"Seeking knowledge is obligatory upon every Muslim"
Prophet Muhammad (PBUH)

Background

The earliest migrants were only interested in finding paid work with the intension to save quickly in order to pay off their borrowed debts. Thus, only a few attempted to learn English.

Progression

After the Immigration Act 1968, Britain saw the arrival of dependent wives and children from Pakistan. Children of school age were enrolled in schools and from the start their minds were prepared that gainful employment was their way forward. Soon after leaving school, they all went into full time employment. The community was still in the process of being established and the status of wealth was considered on a much higher pedestal than academic education.

However, there were a few well-educated and fluent English-speaking men amongst the early arrivals and large numbers of non-English speaking community members were dependent on their assistance for letter reading, writing, completion of tax forms and general advice on immigration matters. Those members of the community played essential roles in providing crucial voluntary service to the members of the community prior to formations of any community organisations in Peterborough. I describe them as the "community champions".

Several elderly members of the community have mentioned that those educated men were inundated with a crowd of people after their work hours and at weekends. One of those men was my late uncle Raja Abdul Majid LLB and according to the earliest city arrivals, he was the first graduate member in the community. He was a practicing lawyer for several years in the city of Mirpur in Azad Jammu and Kashmir before arriving in Peterborough in 1962.

Several years later, the British educated children helped their parents, families and other members of their community with letter writing, reading, form filling, translation, interpreting and with other general clerical work. Many parents felt relieved that their lives had become much more comfortable, thanks to their children's English language and literature skills.

Although many of those pupils now share horrendous stories about their schooling times in Britain, where they were regularly called racist names, intimidated, threatened and physically beaten.

Education is simply the soul of a society as it passes from one generation to another. Gilbert K. Chesterton

Most early Pakistani migrants were either illiterate or had basic primary schooling and only a small number were High School or College Educated in Pakistan. I was interested in ascertaining the causes for their lack of education and after discussions with several elder members of the community, I have concluded with the following assessment:

- Schools were few and far between in the rural villages of Kashmir and in the Northern Punjab. The nearest primary schools were often several kilometres away, high schools were even further away and colleges were only in the cities. The communities lived in small villages without the infrastructure of roads and the walking distances from homes to schools were considered too great for the young children to walk each day.

- The British-Pakistani community heritage areas, inhabitants, were small landowners and dependent on land for their seasonal crops and often-whole families were working on land. Their immediate priorities were to fully concentrate and maximise their efforts on the land. The concept of education meant a potential absence of helping hands.

- Most people did not understand the importance of education and it did not feature highly on people's priority list.

- People were generally poor and simply could not afford to meet their children's education expenses.

Over time, the British-Pakistani community has become more prosperous. A small percentage of parents' awareness of compulsory school education and post-16 higher education in colleges and universities increased. It was not until mid to late 1970's when first members of the British-Pakistani community went to universities. Their numbers were few and one could easily count them on a single hand. The majority of Pakistani parents did not understand either the British education system or the long-term benefits that higher education could bring.

"Education is the most powerful weapon which you can use to change the world" - Nelson Mandela

Way Forward

In the early 1990s, while serving on school governing committees in both primary and secondary schools, I often noticed lack of interest from high number of British-Pakistani parents at the parents' evenings. The school governing committees attempted a various methods and ideas to increase attendances for example arranging interpreters and getting information translated in Urdu but their efforts were often unsuccessful.

In the last decade, the community interests in their children's education has greatly increased and parents are now playing much more important roles by assisting children with homework, attending parents' evenings and making informed choices with their children's GCE's NVQ, A level options and career choices.

However, the community still needs to make further continues progress to bring about the radical important changes and one of the ways would be to actively encourage and support more young people attending universities and that would lead to more academics which will raise the community standing within British society.

My saying on education is that: **"Education is knowledge, knowledge is power and power is authority"**.

"Seek knowledge from the cradle to the grave"
Prophet Muhammad (PBUH)

Children and Young People from the British-Pakistani Community Key Stage Results in Peterborough

In the 2006 Key Stage 1 results, the percentage of children from British-Pakistani heritage achieving level 2 for reading was 65% (12% less than the Peterborough average), in writing, 59% (13% less) and in maths, 71% (14% less).
In Key Stage 2 results, children of British-Pakistani heritage scored 59% in english 16% below the Peterborough average and 57% in maths, 17% below the Peterborough average.
In Key Stage 3 results, with the exception of science, girls of British-

Pakistani heritage improved their performance in english at level 5+, which, at 91%, was above the average for Peterborough. In maths, boys and girls perform considerably worse than the rest of their national cohort. A similar picture is present in science at the end of Key Stage 3.

Despite lower than average performance at Key Stages 1-3, Key Stage 4 achievement of Pakistani heritage pupils was 59% 5+ A*-C which represents a 25% improvement on the 2005 results, above the Peterborough average for all pupils for 2006 and above the national average for Pakistani heritage performance at 57.5%.

"Education is the transmission of civilisation". Will Durant

Peterborough's Children and Young People Future Plan 2007-2010

The progress of identified cohorts of pupils including from the Pakistani heritage performance, this group is identified as being the most statistically significant minority ethnic group in Peterborough, with a record of underperformance.

In the primary phase the (Ethnic Minority Achievement) EMA consultant has worked as part of the Primary Strategy Team to raise achievement. Schools with a large percentage of Pakistani heritage children have been included in the Intensive Support Programme. It is anticipated that the 2007 Key Stage 2 SAT results will show an overall increase for pupils from Pakistani heritage. A good example of partnership work to improve attainment in a specific primary school can be seen in the Beeches. This activity includes the appointment of an English as an Additional Language (EAL) consultant to work collaboratively with the school staff to build assessment systems and staff's ability to secure improvements in outcomes. The DfES 'Excellence and Enjoyment: learning and teaching for bilingual children in the primary years' materials have been incorporated into this programme and also shared with schools with isolated Pakistani heritage pupils. Speaking and listening is seen as important in raising the achievement.

Pakistani heritage pupils remain the most statistically significant ethnic group in Peterborough. Peterborough has a number of growing ethnic groups.

In the 2006 GCSE results, 59% of British-Pakistanis earned more than 5 A*-C grades, which represents a 12% improvement on the 2005 results, above the Peterborough average for all pupils for 2006 and above the national average for British-Pakistani heritage performance at 57.5%. Pakistani heritage remains the most statistically significant ethnic group in Peterborough.

"Education is the key to unlock the golden door of freedom".
George Washington Carver

National GCSE Pass Rates

The table below indicates the GCSE pass rates of British-Pakistani students in comparison with all pupils and the narrowing differences in the attainment gap.

GCSE pass rates for British-Pakistani pupils (5 A-Cs) by year*

Year	British-Pakistani Pupils	All Pupils	Attainment Gap
1993	24%	42%	-18
1995	23%	44%	-21
1997	29%	46%	-17
1999	30%	49%	-19
2001	40%	51%	-11
2003	41.5%	52%	-10.5
2005	48.4%	54.9%	-6.5
2007	53%	59.3%	-6.3
2008	58%	63.5%	-5.3
2009	66.4%	69.8%	-3.04

British-Pakistanis Underrepresented in Universities

British Pakistanis, along with Bangladeshi students, are the most underrepresented in UK universities. This is due to high poverty amongst the British-Pakistani children, which means that less privileged potential students are not making it to universities according to a 2009 government report that reviewed ethnic minorities in higher education.

In 2007/08, the total population of 18-24 year-old British-Pakistanis in the UK was 2.2% but their number at universities was 1.9%.

The review carried out by Race for Opportunity found that black and ethnic minorities in Britain overall are better represented in higher education than their share of the general population. Almost 1.6% (16%) of UK university students are from the black and minority ethnic backgrounds.

The review also found that elite universities (like Oxford and Cambridge) are not properly representing students from black and minority ethnic backgrounds. Only Chinese and mixed ethnicity students were better represented at Oxford.

Black and minority ethnic graduates find it harder to find employment when compared to white students. Just 56.3% of black and minority ethnic students who graduated in 2007-08 found work within a year compared with 66% of white students.

"Live as if you were to die tomorrow and learn as if you were to live forever". Gandhi

City Rankings

In a recent Secondary School National League Table Published Report, Peterborough was ranked 142 out of 151 in terms of pupils gaining five A* to C grades, including English and Maths, in GCSEs taken in 2010. Peterborough pupils overall are more than 10% below the national average in 2010, and the British-Pakistani students are 20% below. In terms of primary schools, Peterborough ranked sixth from bottom in a national league table published in December 2010.

Exemplary Parent

I recently met a local British-Pakistani man and while discussing the importance of education he explained that he values education as the essential requirement in life and shared with me that his two oldest daughters have attended a local private fee paying secondary school. He added it cost him a considerable amount of money annually but their achievements have been well worth the efforts. His financial support has paid real dividends, as both are now attending universities of their choice.

General Information

It is estimated that 25% of the 13,000 Peterborough secondary school pupils do not speak English as their first language. In primary schools, about 33% of school pupils do not speak English as their first language. The five most spoken languages in Peterborough schools are:

1. English
2. Punjabi/ Urdu
3. Polish
4. Portuguese
5. Lithuanian

"Education is our passport to the future, for tomorrow belongs to those people who prepare for it today" Malcolm X

Moving Forward

Parents

Although the British-Pakistani community value education a great deal more than earlier years, but I am of an opinion that more can be achieved, therefore I would recommend the parents take the following action:

- ¤ Attend parent evenings
- ¤ Attend children's sports days
- ¤ Attend school open meetings
- ¤ Actively participate in school fund raising events
- ¤ Assist children with home work
- ¤ Become school governors

In my opinion, parents' active involvement with their children's early formative education will encourage, motivate, and inspire their children to build stronger foundations for their future development and achievements. It reminds me of a famous Chinese saying:

"The journey of 1000 miles must begin with a single step".

I am certain that a parents' interest, support and contribution will send positive vibes/signals to a child that their parents are interested in their education, which will ultimately give them an incentive to work harder, aim higher and go on to achieve greater success in their lives.

Young People

Set your sights on realistic, measurable and achievable school targets. Keep your motivation levels high with effective time management in order to work harder and to accomplish your set goals. Give your best to make your dreams come true. This will inevitably bring joy on your parents and the community and make all of us proud of you and enable you to leave your footprints for future generations to aspire to inspire.

Good luck in all your endeavours................

Lahore Fort – The structure base was built by the Mughal Emperor Akhbar and now a UNESCO World Heritage Site

The Heritage of the Community

Mahmood Hashmi

I conclude the education chapter with my recognition to Mahmood Hashmi (known as Hashmi Sahib) for his innovative work to promote the Urdu language in Peterborough schools. He was employed first Urdu teacher in Peterborough from 1978 to around 1984 by the Cambridgeshire Education Authority. I was one of his pupils at St Paul's School in my GCE/O level in Urdu. Hashmi Sahib also taught Urdu at several other City secondary schools including Jack Hunt, Walton and at Bretton Woods.

He was a well-known and respected figure throughout the country and former editor of the first UK published national Urdu Weekly newspaper 'Mashraq'.

Hashmi Sahib was a softly spoken, gentle and quiet man with a wealth of knowledge and experience, someone I would describe as a true academic.

He graduated with a BA from Punjab University and MA LLB from the prestigious and renowned Aligarh Muslim University before the partition of the Indian sub-continent. He then taught at the Prince of Wales and Amar Singh Colleges in Srinagar in Kashmir State. Later, Hashmi Sahib worked as the Chief Publicity Officer for the new Azad Jammu and Kashmir government.

Whilst teaching Urdu in Peterborough, Hashmi Sahib inspired many young people with motivation, encouragement and with sound advice that an academic education is essential to achieving success in their careers.

I acknowledge that he truly made an impact on my life and that of many other pupils in Peterborough.

Political Contributions

Background

The Peterborough British-Pakistani community has made a considerable political contribution in terms of Councillors and Mayors. Councillors are the elected representatives of the people with important roles and responsibilities at the Local Authorities. They represent the opinions of their constituents regardless of their race, gender, age or class. A proactive Councillor with sound area knowledge can raise the profile of their Ward and fight for better services, as well as securing development and growth funds.

Council Functions

Since Peterborough became a Unitary Authority, the City Council has become responsible for providing all Local Authority provided services. The services range from waste management (bin collection) to the local education authority (LEA) management of both primary and secondary schools and from youth provisions to electoral registration and more.

Kashmiri People

While compiling the political contribution list I have noticed that over the last 50 years the political contribution by the British-Pakistani community in Peterborough has come from people of Kashmiri origin, apart from one newly elected Councillor Nabil Ahmed Shabbir. I cannot provide a valid reason or justification for this except perhaps that the people of Kashmiri origin are more politically aware or it simply relates to the community area numbers game.

The list below gives names of all those people who have made a political contribution to Peterborough after being elected as Councillors by their Ward constituents. Some later went on to serve as Deputy Mayor and Mayor of Peterborough.

Mohammed Hussain

He was the first British-Pakistani in Peterborough to successfully win the Council election in the Central Ward in 1983 as the Labour Party candidate. He subsequently won the next three re-elections as sitting Ward Councillor before stepping down due to ill health.

Mr Hussain is an elder and respected member of the community. He has also served as a Magistrate Justice of Peace (JP) for a number of years and a School Governor. During his working career, he worked for British Rail before retiring as a manager.

Mohammad Ayub Choudhary

He was elected Labour Councillor in 1992 in Central Ward. He subsequently won three re-elections as a sitting Ward Councillor.

Prior to being elected Councillor, his involvement and experience with the community were as Secretary of the Asian Community Association, School Governor and Non-Executive Director of the Hospital Trust. In 2001, Mr Choudhary was shortlisted for a Parliamentary seat. He has since served as the Chairman of a Primary Care Trust for 6 years.

Mr Choudhary has worked for the County Council, the Regional College and currently holds the Directorship of Gladstone District Community Association.

Mohammed Sabeel

He was the first British-Pakistani elected as a Cambridgeshire County Councillor in 1989. He was the Labour Party candidate for Central Ward, served one full term, and has not sought re-election since.

Prior to being elected Councillor his involvement and experience with the community were as an Executive Committee Member of the Pakistan Welfare Association and both Asian Community Association and Asian Youth Club, School Governor, founder member of both the Pakistan Community Association and the Pakistan Youth Association.

Mr Sabeel has worked for the City Council as a Manager of the Gladstone Park Community and Recreation Centre for about 10 years and currently holds a senior position as East Midland Regional Manager for Homeless Link.

Ansar Ali

He was elected Labour Cambridgeshire County Councillor in 1993, for Central Ward. He served one term with an extension as the last County Councillor before Peterborough City Council became a Unitary Authority in 1998. He has not sought re-election since.

Prior to being elected Councillor, his involvement and experience within the community were as a Youth and Community Development Worker and School Governor. Since then he has served as a HM Prison Governor Board of Visitors, Justice of Peace (JP), and as a Non-Executive Director of North West Anglia Health Trust. Mr Ali has also served on the UNISON National Black Members Committee for a number of years. He was founder and the Chairman of Peterborough Muslim Education Trust (PMET), which established Iqra Girls Academy. He is coordinator of the British Friends of Islamgarh Welfare Trust, an Independent Member of Cambridge Police Authority and a former Secretary of Ghousia Mosque Committee.

Mr Ali has worked for the County Council, City Council and South Holland District Council until couple of years ago when he retired from a senior management position after 30 years of service.

Nazim Khan MBE

He was elected Labour Councillor in 1996 in Central Ward. He subsequently won three re-elections as a sitting Councillor. In 2009, once again, he was elected Labour Councillor in the Central Ward.

Prior to being elected Councillor, his involvement and experience with the community were as an Executive Committee member of the Pakistan Welfare Association and Chairman of the Pakistan Community Association. Since he is involved in the community is as a Vice Chairman of a School Governing Committee, leading Regional Trade Unionist in the Transport and the General Workers Union, Chairman of the Gladstone Connect and a member of the Industrial Tribunal Panel.

In 2005, Mr Khan was awarded the honour of Member of the Order of the British Empire (M.B.E) for his services to the community.

Mr Khan works part time for the Pakistan Community Association as the Pre-School Coordinator.

Raja Akhtar Hussain Raja

He was elected Labour Councillor in 1997 in the Central Ward. He subsequently won a couple of re-elections as a sitting Councillor, before defecting to the Conservative Party.

Prior to being elected Councillor, his involvement and the experience within the community were as Treasurer of Ghousia Mosque, School Governor and the Treasurer of the Pakistan Community Association.

Mr Raja works for a Care Agency as a Team Manager.

Mohammed Jamil

He was elected as Labour Councillor in 2001 from the Bretton Ward. He served his one term. Several years later, in 2010, he emerged as the Labour Councillor for the Central Ward.

Prior to being elected Councillor, his involvement and the experience with the community were as a Chairman of a School Governing Committee and member of several Gladstone Connect Committees.

Mr Jamil has worked for the Home Office as a lawyer for a number of years.

Gul Nawaz

He was the first elected Conservative Councillor in 2002 from the West Ward, subsequently winning all of his three re-elections as sitting Councillor.

Since becoming, a Councillor his involvement in the community is as a School governor. Mr Nawaz is presently making his full time commitment to his constituents.

Mohammed Younis

He was the first elected Conservative Councillor in 2002 in the Central Ward. He served one term.

Prior to being elected Councillor his involvement and experience with the community were as a Neighbourhood Watch Scheme Coordinator and a member of the Gladstone Park Management Committee. Mr Younis is self-employed.

Abdul Razaq

He was elected Conservative Councillor in 2004 in the Central Ward. Prior to being elected Councillor, his involvement and experience with the community were as a Vice Chairman of Gladstone District

Community Association, Executive Committee member of the Pakistan Community Association, and Executive Committee member of the Racial Equality Council. Mr Razaq was a member of the Masjid Khadijah Committee.

Since his involvement with the community were as a School Governor and member of the Gladstone Connect. Mr Razaq is Head of Iqra Girls Academy.

Mohammed Sabir

He was elected as Labour Councillor in 2004 in the Central Ward. He served one term.

Prior to being elected Councillor, his involvement and experience with the community were as a Vice Chairman of the Pakistan Community Association and a School Governor. Since his involvement has been the Vice Chairman of the Interfaith Council and remains Vice Chairman of the Pakistan Community Association. Mr Sabir is self-employed.

Mahmood Fazal

He was elected as Conservative Councillor in 2006 in the Central Ward. He served one full term. After becoming a Councillor he was a member of Cambridgeshire Police Authority. Mr Fazal is self-employed.

Zahid Hussain

He was elected as Labour Councillor in 2008 in the Central Ward. He served one term.

Prior to being elected as Councillor his involvement and experiences with the community were as an Executive Committee Member of the Pakistan Community Association. Mr Hussain is self employed.

Mohammed Nadeem

He was elected as Conservative Councillor in the May 2011 elections in the Central Ward. He is a new Councillor and a self-employed.

Nabil Ahmed Shabbir

He was elected Labour Councillor in the May 2011 elections for

EastWard.

Nabil is the youngest ever Councillor from the British-Pakistani community to date.

Former Mayors and Deputy Mayors

- Councillor Mohammed Hussain was the first British-Pakistani to serve as Deputy Mayor of Peterborough in 1989/90 for a year. He was a Labour Councillor. During his term, he assisted with raising funds for the Mayor's chosen charities.

- Councillor Mohammad Ayub Choudhary was the first British-Pakistani to serve as the Mayor of Peterborough in 1996/97 for a year. He was a Labour Councillor. During his term as the Mayor Mohammad Choudhary raised £26,000 for his two chosen charities, UNISEF and Dwarfism Society.

According to Mr Choudhary, while being the first citizen of Peterborough his achievements were;

1. He united all Peterborough multicultural communities.
2. During his Mayor making ceremony, for the first time ever, recitation from the Holy Qur'an was performed inside Peterborough Cathedral.
3. He successfully secured £600,000 from the lottery funds for the Gladstone District Community Association, building extensions/renovations to facilitate community based projects.

- Councillor Raja Akhtar Hussain Raja served as the Deputy Mayor of Peterborough in 2002/03 and he assisted with raising funds for the Mayor's chosen charities. He was a Conservative Councillor.

- The following year in 2004/2005, Councillor Raja Akhtar Hussain Raja served as the Mayor of Peterborough for a year. He was a Conservative Councillor. He was the second British-Pakistani to serve as the Mayor of Peterborough. During his Mayor term, he raised over £20,000 for Sue Ryder and Muscular Dystrophy, his two chosen charities. Mayor fund raising efforts were diverted to concentrate on the Boxing Day Tsunami Appeal Fund.

According to Mr Raja Akhtar while being the first citizen of Peterborough his achievements were;

1. Actively campaigning for the establishment of a university in Peterborough.
2. Lobbied for and supported the new purpose built mosques in Peterborough.
3. Supported and assisted with the proposal of the New City Hospital.

♦ Councillor Gul Nawaz served as the Deputy Mayor of Peterborough in 2008/09. During his term, he assisted with raising funds for the Mayor's chosen charities. He was a Conservative Councillor.

Moving Forward

As someone with two decades of Local Authority experience, I feel I can express my impartial views on this important and often controversial area of the community representation. Before I open the discussion readers, bear in mind millions of people from around the world have given their precious lives to exercise their opinion and have their right to vote. I recommend that we must always use our democratic right to express our views and vote.

I would like to see Councillors being fit for their purpose and remember the saying the 'pen is mightier than the sword' and this is very true.

In my opinion, the qualities of an effective Councillor are that he/she must be a professional, accessible resident of the Ward; pro-active, consistent, caring, accountable, committed to the community and above all has served an apprenticeship on various aspects of community involvement and not become a Councillor for the name sake or additionally dependent on Councillor allowances. Any elected Councillor without prior community experience would spend several years of the learning process.

When electing a Councillor always give preference to the most capable candidate who can represent you and your ward with best interests regardless of their ethnic origins, gender or clan background.

Before the polling day read all political parties leaflets/newsletters and evaluate their local and national policies as well as effective service deliveries and their future proposed commitments.

Cast your vote in a secret and confidential manner. You are not required to disclose your voting pattern to anyone and you can vote whichever candidate you like.

If you were using a postal ballot then I would strongly recommend you do not hand your ballot papers to anyone, regardless whether he is a close friend or an immediate relation. I am aware that occasionally the election circumstances may be beyond our control, but our conduct is in our own power.

My advice to you is always follow the electoral registration office procedures or the Election Returning Officer instructions.

Community Organisations

All citywide community, welfare and cultural organisations operating within the community have served the community timely needs. The committed volunteers who eloquently serve large dependent members of the community must be applauded for their time and commitment. At one time majority of the earliest arrivals in Peterborough did not understand the British processes and were heavily reliant on community organisations for regular assistance with immigration, education, welfare rights and employment.

The organisations, which met Peterborough City Council's required criteria, by submitting, annual general meeting minutes along with a copy of their annual statement of accounts, received an annual grant to meet running costs.

According to the members of the community, several organisations were much more active and served the community in greater numbers. The majority of the listed community organisations are no longer functioning. However, those organisations with good democratic foundations, sound structures and with commitments, along with desired drive to serve the community are still functioning after many years.

Pakistan National Association

The Pakistan National Association was the first Pakistani association to form in Peterborough in the early 1960s, after some leading members of the community recognised the urgent need for a community association to assist and provide support to the largely dependent members of the community. The purpose of the association was to have a collective and recognised community voice. To represent and speak on behalf of the community as well as challenging the Local

Authority and other public service providing agencies.

It is no longer a functioning association but while it was operational, the services it provided were advice and support to the local community in welfare rights, taxation enquiries, and employment and immigration matters.

"The heritage of the community recognised and complements the earliest pioneers for taking the timely initiative with the best community interest at heart by forming this community organisation"

Pakistan Welfare Association (PWA)

This welfare association formed in the early 1970s. For a long period, PWA was the sole representative of the British-Pakistani community in Peterborough. It was the only association consulted by local the voluntary and statutory agencies. PWA is an affiliate of the PCA.

The association's activities are to provide advice and support to the local community in welfare rights, religious and cultural needs, housing, education, immigration and nationality status and it helped celebrate the Pakistan Independence Day for many years.

Gladstone District Community Association (GLADCA)

This Community association (commonly known as GLADCA) was formed in 1972. The association is one of the oldest functioning associations in Peterborough. The association's office is at the 316-318 Gladstone Street Peterborough.

The services GLADCA provides to the local community are welfare, community care, housing, education, employment & training (consumer & general), benefits, ESL classes for women, citizenship courses and more. They specialise in dealing with immigration & nationality, asylum, visa applications, work permits, appeals and indefinite leave to remain orders in the UK.

Asian Community Association (ACA)

The Asian Community Association was formed in the late 1970s to manage the newly acquired Asian Cultural Centre on Lincoln Road, New England, after years of negotiations with Peterborough City Council about providing the Asian community with their own community centre, where community and cultural functions could be held, as well as providing sports and recreational facilities for the young people of South Asian communities. Peterborough City Council purchased an old church building and renovated it into a small community centre.

The association's committee membership included representatives of all Peterborough South Asian communities. The committee functioned well until 1989 when the Council opened the new £1.2 million Gladstone Park Community and Recreation Centre on Bourges Boulevard.

In the early 1990s, the association formally dissolved after the Asian Cultural Centre building was handed back to Peterborough City Council. This was due to the centre requiring extensive updating repairs to maintain the building for public use but the required funds were not available to undertake this renovation work. The Council has since reconverted the building back into a church.

Whilst the Asian Community Association was a functioning association, it was responsible for the day-to-day management of the Asian Cultural Centre. This ensured that the community Centre was readily available for the maximum usage as well as providing sports and recreational facilities for the young people of the Peterborough South Asian communities.

Asian Youth Club (AYC)

This youth club was established soon after the formation of the Asian Community Association. The aim of the Asian Youth Club was to facilitate the needs of the young people of the community. The youth club operated well for about 10 years before relocating into the newly built Gladstone Park Community and Recreation Centre and was renamed the Pakistan Youth Association.

The Asian Youth Club provided sports and recreation facilities for 12 - 18 year olds of the South Asian communities. Youth workers carried out face-to-face interaction with young people by, listening, gaining mutual trust and confidence, providing knowledge and information, equipping them with skills and preparing them for adulthood.

British Pakistani Welfare Association

This welfare association formed in 1980 and it was a well-organised and active association that served the community needs for a good number of years. It was an affiliate of the PCA and is no longer a functioning association.

The activities the association covered while operational were; welfare rights, religious and cultural needs, social development, employment, housing, education, benefits, immigration, nationality and other general areas.

Anglo Pakistani ex- Servicemen Association

This servicemen's association was formed in the 1980s with the aim of providing services to the ex-Anglo British-Pakistani servicemen. It served the community well for many years and was an affiliate of the PCA. The association is now defunct.

Whilst operational, the activities covered were welfare rights, religious and cultural needs, social development, community employment projects, housing, education, employment, benefits, immigration and nationality.

Pakistan Kashmir Welfare Association

This welfare association was formed in 1980 and served the community for many years and was an affiliate of the PCA. It is now defunct. While operational, the Association met on the first Thursday of every month at 7.30pm and every weekend (either Sunday or Saturday) at 2.00 - 4.00pm.

The activities covered by the association whilst it was running were: serving and advising on immigration, passport services, Department of Health and Social Security (DHSS) benefit provisions both locally and nationally, the role of the police, religion, legal problems and translations and interpretations.

Youth Education Committee

This committee was specifically set up to deal with British-Pakistani youth education issues on a citywide basis, was an affiliate of the PCA, and is no longer a functioning committee.

The committee activities while operational were to provide support, advice and assistance to British-Pakistani parents with any education issues concerning their children.

Pakistan Community Association (PCA)

This association was formed in 1988 with support from the Peterborough City Council. It is an umbrella association made up of eight smaller cultural and community groups, plus two mosques Faizan-e-Madinah and Jamia Ghousia.

The main aim of the association is to unite the Peterborough British-Pakistani community and to manage the multi-million pound purpose built Gladstone Park Community Recreation Centre. After 23 years of Peterborough British-Pakistani community representation, the association is still functioning and operates from the Crossroads Learning Centre in Gladstone Street. PCA is a registered charity and manages a well attended and a popular pre-school playgroup.

The activities of the PCA are information, welfare rights, religious and cultural needs, social development, community employment projects, youth information and workshops, homework clubs, a youth club, training and courses at the Crossroads Centre.

Pakistan Youth Association (PYA)

PYA formed in 1989 after the relocation of youth provision from the Asian Cultural Centre to a new purpose built Gladstone Park Community Recreation Centre.

The Pakistan Youth Association is the sole citywide representative of British-Pakistani young people in Peterborough. It is one of the affiliates of the PCA and after 22 years, the Peterborough City Council's Connexions Services directly manage youth provisions are still going strong and youth activity sessions are well attended.

PYA activities are based on the Young People's Curriculum providing knowledge and information, allowing opportunities for young people to enjoy and achieve, to be healthy, stay safe, and make a positive contribution to aid their personal development and achievement. Physical health helps develop confidence in a healthy lifestyle. It offers a safe, secure provision of positive activities for young people to prepare them for adulthood.

Moving Forward

All citywide British-Pakistani community functioning organisations must work with common objectives and the best interests of the community which are achieved by working collectively, with excellent flow of communications, meeting regularly to avoid any confusion or misunderstanding, by sharing information with a "live and let live" strategy and by providing community reflective services.

The organisations must co-exist and not undermine each other's position by individually claiming to represent the whole community. All organisational core concept values must be based on win-win principles for the community and by utilizing and pooling the community resources effectively.

The organisations must be united by their ideals instead of divided by their differences.

The sole purpose of the Pakistan Community Association (PCA) formation was to unite all Peterborough British-Pakistani community operating welfare, cultural and other groups under one united umbrella association and that to represent the voice of the community. Therefore, it is vitally important to recognise the PCA as the overall representative of the community. Likewise, the other community-operated groups have the responsibility to support the association.

Cultural Conflicts

Introduction

This leads to a more difficult and rather complex aspect of the community culture. These are controversial and adverse topics, which the British-Pakistani community view as their very own cultural and traditional issues and do not openly, like discussing outside their own community. I have briefly touched on some of the most important cultural conflicts issues; however, the truth is that each topic is so complex it could potentially have its own lengthy heading.

Cultural or Religious

An important issue, which needs to be highlighted, is the confusion by the indigenous and other UK communities on the differences between British-Pakistani community traditional values, customs and religious beliefs. I am certain that there are some areas, which even members of the British-Pakistani community are unsure or often fail to distinguish whether they are traditions or religious issues. Both British media and other communities occasionally spread inaccurate and misleading information about the British-Pakistani community by labelling traditions as religious issues and vice versa.

Negative Discussions

Another area, which concerns me, is that at almost every gathering discussion are based on the negative aspects of Pakistan. My suggestion to those people is to be mindful of Pakistan's image amongst other communities. We can complain about the problems forever but instead, think about the constructive solutions.

Parental Expectations

In recent years, the British-Pakistan community has been experiencing radical cultural changes, specifically with their children. All parents have elevated and glowing expectations of their children in terms of being respectful, having successful careers and above all being good human beings. Whereas the vast majority of young people are often confused and torn between the only British ways of life, they know and the Pakistani culture/tradition their parents often preach about to them. Many young people are also stumbling across the language barrier as a small percentage of young people speak limited to no Punjabi or

Urdu. The language difficulties along with the lack of cultural understanding are resulting in many young people abstaining from family and community gatherings like wedding receptions, birthday parties and other community events. I would describe these problems as the 'generation gap'; these along with cultural changes are leading to family and social discord.

Lack of Respect

The British-Pakistani community values its culture, traditions as norms, which the community has practiced for millennia. Whilst the community was small in Peterborough parents maintained the traditions and culture, latterly sadly, one cannot fail to notice how many positive cultural aspects with strong religious elements of our lives are disappearing, the loving, caring head of the family status which parents and grandparents always revered. Today, a sizeable minority of young people do not respect their parents' views and often describe them old fashioned and outdated. When parents try to hold conversation with young people, they become eruptive, disrespectful and abusive towards them. In my opinion, these issues could be connected to the following reasons:

- ♯ Fathers working long unsociable hours and unable to spend quality time with children.
- ♯ Lack of opportunities to establish close father-child relationships whilst children were growing up.
- ♯ No direct influence on their children's upbringing.
- ♯ These problems may be linked to changing society and times.

Respect, acquired knowledge and wisdom of the elderly are also fading fast. I remember the times when an elder person entered into the house or a room and all the young people would stand up to greet them with esteem and drop everything gave their full attention.

Arranged Marriages

Traditionally almost all marriages in the British-Pakistani community were arranged in families, area or within clan members but recently, there has been a cultural shift amongst young people with reluctance to follow their ancestor's footsteps of marrying in families or marry in Pakistan and in traditional arranged marriage ceremonies. Many young people's actions are leading to clashes in thinking and to severe resentment in their families, including frictions and long-term

The Heritage of the Community

complicated family fallouts. However, in recent years, a high percentage of parents' attitudes are changing and they have started to embrace the timely related changes and often permit the wishes of their children to avoid divisions and unhappy family situations. There are still a number of parents who find the cultural changes of young people difficult to accept, which leads to irritation and divisions.

Mixed Marriages

I acknowledge that a small percentage of the British-Pakistani community men and an even smaller parentage of women are marrying outside their community. Many of mixed heritage marriages tend to dissolve within the first few years and often their given reasons are cultural and religious differences, however I do admit that a small percentage of these mixed heritage marriages do succeed.

Lack of Responsibilities

The complaints I hear from fathers is that their sons are not committed to assuming full responsibilities or not earning a decent living wage to maintain their independent living. I think there is a certain element of truth in their concerns. We have to remember Pakistani born fathers' cultural upbringing was different to their British born and Western culture influenced sons. Both generations of people are experiencing different lifestyles and one cannot compare them. Although many young people have some sense of affinity and linkage with Pakistan, it remains the country of heritage. Fathers have often gone through experiences of hardships in their lives and strongly believe that hard work is the essential key to success and they are accustom to living a life on what they can afford. I best describe their lives as "live to earn". In contrast, their sons' perception about life is to take it easy and enjoy themselves, which I describe as "earn to live".

I stress that one of the ways to make young people more responsible is to delegate them smaller, easier and much more manageable tasks at a young age and gradually increase the level of responsibilities, as they grow older. This will inevitably build up their capacities, increase their awareness, self-confidence and accountabilities.

Appreciation for Parents

Young people need also to express their appreciation and be thankful to their parents for their lifetime hard work with their thoughts and intentions of making their children's lives comfortable. If any young person is in disagreement me then he/she can ask any member of the community attempting a fresh start in Britain today and you will discover they are finding life a huge struggle. This is connected with expensive property prices, high private rents, and limited employment prospects, which are often on short-term contracts making it virtually impossible for any newcomer to step on the property ladder.

Drugs, Crime and Prison

In the last decade, the issue of drugs has considerable been on rise amongst the younger members of the community. Their first exposure often comes after leaving school without any formal qualifications, and then encountering severe problems in gaining paid work ultimately resulting in becoming caught up in the world of drugs.

The young people involvements initially start as consumers, which later compelled with the temptations to get rich quick often changes to both consumers and suppliers. Their actions are distressing their parents and having a detrimental impact on the British-Pakistani community. Many parents feel confused as to why their sons have become involved with drugs and unsure as to whom they should approach for advice or help. They feel powerless and some even send their sons on a long 'holiday' to Pakistan in hope that change in environment and will lead to their cessation in drug use. The other main worry their parents have is the possibility of police drug raids and if any raids do take place, it brings embarrassment on family and the community.

Many young people are addicted and dependent on drugs and it is a costly habit forcing them to turn to crime to feed their addiction. This inevitably results in a steadily increase in crime within the British-Pakistani community's residential areas. Their unlawful activities lead to police prosecutions and ultimately to prison. In 1991, there were 1,959 Muslims in UK prisons, and 8 years on in 1999, the number had more than doubled, with 4,335 in prison. The latest 2011 figures state there are currently 10,300 Muslim prisoners in England and Wales and that is 12% of the total prison population. The total UK prison population is about 85,000. I am aware that these figures include a proportion of newly converted Muslim prisoners who have embraced Islam whilst in prison. The majority of Muslim prisoners are below 30 years of age and unfortunately, once they have criminal record most experience that it is virtually impossible to find paid employment and without much of choice high percentages of released prisoners reoffend and quickly find themselves behind bars again.

Positive Changes

I will conclude this chapter on a positive note. In recent years, there has been a noticeable change in the community, especially on marriages and on the father's involvements with children as:

◊ Fewer family marriages and more choice-based arranged marriages have started to take place in the community.
◊ Fewer marriages are now organised in Pakistan. More marriages are now arranged within the UK British-Pakistan community.
◊ More fathers play active role by spending quality time and influencing their children's upbringing.

The Facts

A sense of identity for many young Muslims is formed from a mixture of experiences within the family, the community, educational institutions, and religion. Yet many young Muslims feel they have an inadequate grasp of their own heritage and history, something to use as a reference to balance out the other influences in their lives. Young Muslims are concerned about the way they are understood by the public (non-Muslim and Muslim) and

how they are portrayed in the media.

◆ 31% of British Muslims agreed that Imams are out of touch with the views of young Muslims. (MORI poll, 2005).
◆ Discussion between young people on the Muslim Youth Helpline, a confidential helpline for young Muslims, is including topics such as ineffective services for young Muslims; discontent over foreign policy and the difficulties of integrating when people have the dual identity of being British and a Muslim i.e. of neither being wholly of one nationality or the other.
◆ 62% of Muslim youth, aged 16 - 24 say they have as much in common with non-Muslims as Muslims, compared to 71% of 55+ year olds.

- 37% of 16 - 24 year olds would prefer to live under Shari'ah Law compared to 71% of 55+ year olds.
- 64% of 16 - 24 year olds would prefer Muslim women to choose to wear the veil, compared to 28% of 55+ year olds.

Final Thoughts

Our community is our identity and we must continue to preserve this. However, we also need to recognise it is inevitable further time related accelerating cultural changes would happen in our community. The community must be prepared and show their flexibility to embrace any future changes with peace of mind, to remain strong, cultural, and prosperous.

British Mosques

A recent study found that British mosques were dominated by foreign-trained Imams thus leaving young Muslims at the mercy of radicals. 97% of Imams in Britain's mosques are from overseas despite the majority of Muslims in Britain being born in the UK. The study also found 44% of mosques do not hold the sermons of the main Friday Prayers in English.

The study said that nearly half of Britain's mosques do not provide facilities for women, "depriving half the community of access to public spaces". The study said. Foreign-trained Imams are poorly paid, and with limited proficiency in English and are ill equipped to navigate Britain's complex liberal and multi-faith society. They have neither the freedom of being at the mercy of mosque management committees dominated by first generation elders, nor the capacity to promote an Islam true to authentic Islamic values.

Religious Leadership

By failing to reach out to young British Muslims, radicals have started to influence the mindset of the young who are without a voice in mosques. Many young people are looking elsewhere for religious guidance and continue to be drawn in by articulate hardliners who offer an alternative narrative, cause and social space.

Young People's Discontentment

Time after time young people from the British-Pakistani community raise this question and ask who represents their views (also highlighted I Muslim Youth Helpful survey) as they often feel ignored by the establishments, agencies, politicians, and by the government. The area that frustrates young people most is Britain's stance on foreign policy as they view our current policies as unfair, unbalanced, unequal and dishonest. Most young people strongly believe that if Britain follows a course that is more systematic and principled then in the long term Britain will gain more respect around the world.

Moving Forward

1. An overwhelming member of the British-Pakistani community feels that they belong to Britain.
2. For mosques to become more effective and inclusive of all sections of the community they need to include women and young people in their management committees so that that their mosque is sufficiently meeting the needs of the Muslim communities.
3. Work in partnership with government set agencies aimed at the supporting young people.
4. The mosque committee members need to be aware that they are responsible in making sure their services are connecting with the community and young people.
5. The mosque committees must setup its framework to work in a joined up approach with other voluntary and statutory agencies.
6. Mosques must share their space with community organisations/groups, schools and by opening their doors more often to non-Muslim people.

The world famous Taj Mahal

The Heritage of the Community

The Ways Forward for the Community

"Even God does not change the condition of any community unless community is prepared for change" Sir Dr Allama Muhammed Iqbal

The British-Pakistani community is a friendly, cultural, hardworking and proud community. If the community wants to achieve further progress by become a leading British community then one of the ways forward for the members of the community would be to become more involved in their vicinity in:

- ✓ Neighbourhood Watch Schemes
- ✓ Playgroup Committees
- ✓ Local Practice Committees
- ✓ Play Centre Committees
- ✓ NHS Area Panels
- ✓ Community or Resident Associations
- ✓ Community Centre Management Committees
- ✓ Youth Club Committees
- ✓ Police Area Panel Committees
- ✓ Area based Committees

Community activists and Councillors have the duty to encourage and identify new and emerging young talent. These people who have drive and a real commitment along with an ethos of adherence to working with the community to sustain its progression with strategies, which are grounded in outcomes that are realisable, practical and fit for the 21st century and beyond. Remember great communities are those, which produce great people.

Integration

The British-Pakistani community needs to be seen as an active and vibrant part of British Society rather than living segregated parallel lives. We must be part of mainstream British culture to succeed. The word you often hear is integration. Younger members of the community resent this word and simply think it means a one-sided focus on minority communities. There is also a widespread view in the community regardless of their efforts; that the indigenous community will never accept them as being truly British. Some members are also very critical about the low levels of awareness and lack of interest in the indigenous community regarding minority communities and cultures. Other members recognise that their community will have to compromise parts of their culture in the process to integrate. I personally welcome the vision of integration as a mutual two way forward process for the community. Assimilation, however, is completely unacceptable. We must survive with our own definitive intact identity as the British-Pakistani community.

Political Parties

I suggest the way forward for the British-Pakistani community is to abandon the Pakistani political parties' affiliation in Britain and instead concentrate fully on British politics. We are part of British Society and to win our community more support and become real stakeholders in the mainstream we need to raise the community profile in a positive way to become empowered, successful, important, predominant community. I recommend joining the main UK political parties and by playing an active role to win more influence and recognition. I am certain that the British-Pakistani community's greater participation in the political party's structures would lead to more members of the community becoming Councillors, Members of the Welsh Assembly, Scottish Parliament, UK and European Parliaments.

My recommendations are that you always read the manifesto pledges of all political parties, this can be accessed via internet or alternatively contact their local party representatives' for hard copies, in the UK National Parliamentary and the European Parliament elections.

Miscellaneous Committees

I commend the British-Pakistani community to play an active part in cross sections of panels, trusts, boards and committees, which are empowered to make vital policymaking decisions and considered as the driving forces behind British Society. These may include:

- ➢ Police Committees
- ➢ Health Trusts Committees
- ➢ Tribunal Committees
- ➢ Local Authority Committees
- ➢ Boards
- ➢ Magistrates

The world is interconnected by becoming a global village and we need to create a mechanism, which will enable the community to develop further and to remember, change is inevitable and constant.

Trade Unions

Trade unions possess powerful voices. Some of the largest British Trade Unions have more than 1.5 million members. Unions still carry influence and the national media and the political parties often hear their messages loud and clear. This could be another avenue for the British-Pakistani community to be noticed and play its part to win more support. Once again, I recommend that you start your participation at the lower level by learning and increasing your knowledge of the policies, structures and the decision making processes at your work place or local branch by becoming a work place representative, steward, branch officer, then later progress onto area, regional and national committee levels.

Very Important People (VIP) Cultural

While discussing the empowerment topic, I will also appeal to the members of the British-Pakistani community to stop the VIP culture of hospitalities for visiting Pakistani politicians. They often visit the UK on money spinning ventures and most of these politicians are wealthy in their own right and not dependant on our community for support. Our communities must distance ourselves from these individuals. In my opinion, they are often incompetent of performing the duties for which they are elected. When meeting some visiting politicians it reminded me of President Kennedy's famous political quote, "Ask not what your country can do for you, but what you can do for your country".

The Way Forward

We need to look ahead and become a forward thinking community. We must recognise our British-Pakistani enriched heritage is an enormous strength for our community. My recommendations are not beyond our reach.

I truly believe that with sprits of change, if the community implement any of my proposals, it will strengthen the foundations of the community further and bring it to the forefront alongside with other leading and successful British communities.

The changes would be positive, beneficial and everlasting, remember those communities, which are not prepared to change are left behind.

Bearing in mind, the challenges ahead is long and arduous as a community we must be prepared remain focus and not lose sight.

Community Health Issues

This chapter is included with a heavy heart as in recent years our British-Pakistani community has suffered so much grief with the tragic deaths of young men in their 20s and 30s who had so much zest for life and who are sadly no longer with us. The whole community endures these premature deaths with sorrow and my condolences are with their families.

At several recent National Health Service (NHS) meetings in the community, I question the state of our young people's health and asked what are NHS strategies on young people who are either hard to engage or hard to reach. The responses I received were like many other services providers, they have enormous demanding pressures on their services and recommend that young people of the community must book an annual health check up; this will enable the health professional to detect any health problems at an early stage and treat them.

I personally think it is a positive suggestion and a way forward. I stress you follow the instructions of the medical professionals, as they are the most qualified and best-placed people to provide you the advice.

Remember that an average life expectancy in the Central Ward is about 10 years lower than the average life of residents living in Newborough.

Youth Provisions

Introduction

In the late 1970s, the Asian Community Association was formed to manage the newly acquired Asian Cultural Centre building on Lincoln Road, New England. The association also facilitated youth activities for all young people of Peterborough's South Asian Communities.

The community centre building was an old church converted into a community centre with old wooden floors and very basic facilities. The centre consisted of two halls, one hall had a badminton court and used as the main activity area of the centre and second hall was much smaller, it was used for table tennis and other small games. There were four other small rooms and one of the rooms was for management committee meetings. Another room was an office. One room was used as a pool table room and the fourth room was used for loose weights, benches & bars amongst other exercise apparatus. The building had a separate kitchen.

Asian Cultural Centre Building at Lincoln Road, New England

The association committee membership included representatives of all the Peterborough South Asian communities. In the early 1990s, the association was officially dissolved after the Asian Cultural Centre management committee handed back the building to Peterborough City Council, as the building required extensive modernisation repairs in order to maintain its usage and sufficient levels of funds were not made available to carry out the essential work. The Council has since converted the building back to a church.

Asian Youth Club (AYC)

This youth club was established soon after the formation of the ACA management committee in the late 1970's. The aim of the Youth Club was to serve the needs of the younger people of the South Asian communities. The club operated three evening sessions a week on Monday, Wednesday and Friday from 7.00 pm until 9.00 pm.; all sessions were well attended by the young people.

The youth club produced some excellent, high standard badminton players and played a team in the county badminton league. The team won several league divisions and was renowned for playing skilful and fast badminton. The respective team played for approximately 7-8 years before a lack of interest led to members withdrawing team from the league.

The AYC facilitated sports and recreation facilities for 12-18 year old youths. Youth Workers carried out face-to-face interaction with young people by listening and gaining mutual trust and confidence, providing knowledge and information, and preparing young people for adulthood.

Location

The main problem was the location of the Asian Cultural Centre building as it was situated in the neighbouring New England Area. At that time, the area was considered unsafe for young people to walk during the evenings for fear of being racially abused or attacked.

Relocation

The Asian Youth Club operated well for about 10 years by serving the needs of the young people before relocating into the newly built Gladstone Park Community Centre Recreation Centre and was renamed the Pakistan Youth Association.

Background

I feel it is important to highlight the history of the Gladstone Park Community Recreation Centre. After the Asian Cultural Centre had fulfilled the community needs for approximately 10 years, the community had outgrown the centre requirement facilities in size, location and outdated building.

Several years earlier, some local community activists opened discussions with the Peterborough City Council to provide the community with a purpose built community recreation centre, centrally located, easily accessible and within the community. The negotiations continued for several years and progress was at a standstill, which frustrated many young people of the British-Pakistani community and a small element became disillusioned by feeling deprived from the essential sports and recreation facilities.

In 1987, in a state of desperation, young people from all over the Gladstone Area assembled peacefully to protest on Taverners Road and later moved over to the Bourges Boulevard to raise awareness for a new purpose built community and youth recreation centre. Shortly after the police arrived on the scene and attempted to escort the young people away from the road, they refused to move, which resulted in several young people being arrested by police and later released without any charges.

When the police failed to persuade the young protesters to move on and on the request of young people, police contacted the Peterborough City Council Leader Councillor Charles Swift OBE, who appeared on the scene and appealed to the young people to disperse. They refused to move and insisted on the provision for a new community centre and asked Councillor Swift for a commitment. To resolve the issue quickly and peacefully, he made a commitment with the young people that a new purpose built community centre with youth facilities would be built in 12-18 months time in the Gladstone Area, which will meet the young people and the community needs adequately.

Councillor Swift immediately delegated the task to the Senior Council Officers to carry out feasibility studies on all possible sites in the Gladstone Area. All parties involved agreed with the current Gladstone Park Community Recreation Centre site and discussions opened on the size and the facilities required by the community. The building costs were estimated to be over one million pounds. Peterborough City Council did not have surplus reserves to build a community centre of this size, and ended up negotiating a deal with a third-party contractor. The agreement was that the company will construct the Bayard Place building in Broadway on Council own land and lease the building to council for a number of years and in return, the company would build the Gladstone Park Community Recreation Centre.

Gladstone Park Community Recreation Centre

Work commenced in 1988 and cost £1.2 million. The new premises adequately meet the needs of young people and the British-Pakistani community provisions. The centre was opened by Councillor Charles Swift the leader of the Council in July 1989.

Acknowledgement

"The heritage of the community must acknowledge the radical spirits of young people for leading the campaign and by playing a decisive role to raise the community centre plight to the wider communities".

New Community Facilities

In 1989, soon after the opening of the Gladstone Park Community Centre, Pakistan Youth Association (PYA) block booked three evening sessions a week, Monday, Wednesday and Friday, two sessions for young males and one session for young females. PYA membership increased massively with an excitement from the young people about the new indoor 5-a-side football facilities, four badminton courts, and volleyball, and cricket practice nets and provision for other sports activities. The centre provided excellent tailor-made facilities for the young people and served the needs of the British-Pakistani community.

Hobson Adventure Centre

In 1990s, youth sessions were also operated from Hobson's Adventure Play Centre located on the Cromwell Road. The centre was used by 8-14 years old, children during the daytime. The building was not suitable for the older age members. The centre quickly became overcrowded but at least it provided a place for young people to gather during the cold winter months, kept them warm, and safely off the street as well as offering sports facilities.

In the early 2000 in a Health and Safety inspection, the Hobson Centre building was deemed unsafe and the City Council authorised its forthwith demolition. Hobson was the only building, which provided youth provision for the younger people living in the lower part of the Gladstone Area. The demolition of the Hobson Centre meant depriving young British-Pakistani people from participating in any physical sports, recreation or social interaction activities. A decade later, the demolition-building site still stands vacant and young people continue to miss out.

Since the loss of the building, several alternative arrangements have been put in place for the trials and tribulations to facilitate the needs of the young people residing in that part of the Gladstone Area. These consist of:

➢ Use of Astro-turf football pitches at Stanground, Werrington, Peterborough Town, Thomas Deacon Academy and the Embankment.
➢ A temporary youth club operated from a small community building at Cobden Street.

Area Divide

Sadly, it is a well know fact that there is a territorial divide amongst some young members of the British-Pakistani community between the upper end and the lower end of the Gladstone Area. The division point is Taverners Road. It is incredibly difficult to believe that a small number of young people living in both sections of the Gladstone Area, do not freely interact. They have a sort of pride in their respective areas and both areas' young people know each other well. I think it all stems from which primary schools they have attended (either Beeches or Gladstone Primary), but in recent years there has been positive changes that the situation is gradually improving. There are no division amongst the adult members of the British-Pakistani community living in both sides of the Gladstone Area.

Moving Forward

The community must make efforts to listen and understand the views and the opinions of young people as an important asset and as potentially future community leaders. Any talented young sportsperson need to be encouraged and nourished to make their dream a reality. Their families could facilitate this by providing financial and logistical support and by making sure young people are making informed choices. Bearing in mind that everyone is talented in some way but the hardest task is being able to identify and remember not every young person is academically gifted. Parents must evaluate their children's strengths and act as a catalyst to fulfil their potential.

I would like to see more unity and cooperation amongst the young people of the community. They must view unity as strength and divisions as weakness.

Sports Achievements

Ajaz Akhtar is the most successful British-Pakistani cricketer in Peterborough. Ajaz made his debut for Cambridgeshire in the 1990 Minor Counties Championship against Staffordshire. From 1990 to the present day, he has represented the county in 143 Minor Counties Championship matches. He also represented the county in 56 MCCA Knockout Trophy matches from 1991 to the present day. He is the current Cambridgeshire captain.

Ajaz also represented Cambridgeshire in List-A cricket, where he made his debut in that format of the game against Kent in the 1991 NatWest trophy.

From 1991 to 2004, he represented the county in 16 List-A matches, with his final List-A appearance coming in the 2004 Cheltenham & Gloucester Trophy against Northamptonshire in1991 NatWest Trophy. From 1991 to 2004, he represented the county in 16 List-A matches, with his final List-A appearance coming in the 2004 Cheltenham & Gloucester Trophy against Northamptonshire.

Sports teams connected to the Asian Youth Club or the Pakistan Youth Association or members represented youth club in a sports competitions.

- Asian Youth Club football team played in the Sunday league for about 12 years.
- Asian Youth Club badminton team played in the County league for many years and won several league divisions.
- PYA's football team under-15s played in the Sunday league.
- Asian Youth Club cricket team was the winners of several under-16 national cricket tournaments.
- Member of Asian Youth Club badminton team finished runner-up in under-19 national badminton tournament.
- Asian Youth Club won a regional under-16 five-a-side football tournament.

Pak Azad

Pak Azad Cricket Club is the longest and most successful British-Pakistani community competitive cricket team playing in the local Peterborough League.

The team was established in 1979 by a then young Muzaffar-ul-Hassan in consultation with other local community talented cricketers. He became team captain and ever since he has fulfilled his responsibilities well by being team organiser, motivator and the driving force behind the success of the Pak Azad Cricket Club.

Three decades later, the Pak Azad is still going strong and with competitive sportsmanship spirits, the team play in Spar 20 over Mid-Week league and according to Muzaffar Pak Azad is hoping to join the weekend league again in the near future.

Under the leadership of Muzaffar-ul-Hassan, the Pak Azad Cricket has won many competitions including the prestigious Jadika cup.

Positive Role Models for Young People

Introduction

It is difficult to identify a single person in the Peterborough British-Pakistani community with a unified positive role model status. However, the young people have viewed a number of people as positive community role models at different times.

Feedback

The selections of names are from my discussions, the feedback from young people used the Asian Youth Club and the Pakistan Youth Association facilities. The name order list is based on the popularity of young people and their comments were that they respect, appreciate and admire these people and few even desired to follow in the footsteps of these positive role models.

Raja Sakandar Khan

He is a man who stands out from the rest in Peterborough. He arrived in Britain at a young age from Pakistan and attended both local primary and secondary schools. He has lived in Central Ward all his life.

Sakandar comes from the Mirpur district in Kashmir, although since the building of the Mangla Dam his family relocated to the outskirts of Faisalabad city in the Pakistani province of Punjab.

Sakandar became interested in boxing at a young age (it was the time when the great Muhammad Ali was at his peak in fitness and success) and trained as an amateur boxer.

From his teenage years, he openly expressed his personal and often radically outspoken views, which won him a great deal of respect from the young people and he became the unofficial spokesperson for young people in the community.

With time, he strengthened his social contacts with other Peterborough citywide communities and established connections, with the British-Pakistani community throughout Britain.

Due to his influence, direct style of speaking and mediation skills, he plays an important role in resolving many community conflicts and thanks to his balanced views; final decisions are often acceptable to all sides.

Sakandar has been self-employed all his working life, managing various businesses.

Because of his time efforts and continues involvement with the young people of the community, he is well liked admired and respected by young people.

Mohammed Sabeel

He arrived in Peterborough from the Mirpur district in Kashmir at a young age and attended a secondary school. He has lived in Central Ward all his life.

Sabeel was amongst the young founding members of the Asian Youth Club in the late 1970's and he was an active supportive member of the Youth Club management committee.

In 1989, he was appointed the first Gladstone Park Community & Recreation Centre Manager by Peterborough City Council. Pakistan Youth Association was one of the main users of the centre. Sabeel established close connections with the PYA management committee and as well as the centre using members. PYA had a large membership with average session attendances of around 100 young people. Due to his daily connection, the young people looked up to him with respect as a figurehead and a positive role model.

Ansar Ali

He arrived in Britain from the district of Mirpur in Kashmir at a young age and attended local secondary school. He has lived in Central Ward all his life.

Ansar was amongst the founding members of the Asian Youth Club and became a voluntary youth worker in the late 1970's. In 1980, he was appointed the first Youth Leader In-Charge of the Asian Youth Club. In the mid 1980s, he was employed full time Project Leader at the Asian Cultural Centre and later worked for Peterborough City Council as the Community Development Worker.

Due to his work with young people, Ansar became well known and respected amongst the young people of the community.

Raja Tahir Masood

He arrived in Britain from the district of Mirpur in Kashmir at the age of 14 and attended a local secondary school. He was a resident of Central Ward for most of his life.

In 1980 at the age of 16, Tahir became a voluntary Youth Worker at the Asian Youth Club. Several years, later he was appointed Youth leader In-Charge. In the late 1980s, Peterborough City Council employed him as the Community Development Worker based at the Gladstone Park Community Recreation Centre.

Tahir has worked with the young people from the British- Pakistani community as a Youth Worker for almost 30 years. According to him, "working with young people is one of his life passions and it gives him a great deal of satisfaction".

Young people respect him, value his face-to-face interaction contribution, look up to him and affectionately call him Uncle T, shortened for Tahir.

Zahid Masaud

He is a Peterborough born British-Pakistani man who has lived in Central Ward all his life. He was educated at the local primary and the secondary schools.

While growing up in the city, he used the PYA's youth facilities and for last 10 years, Zahid has been a full time Youth Worker covering the whole of the Gladstone Area and being responsible for youth clubs, detached work, schools and working with other agencies.

Zahid is well known with young people and they respect him by appreciating his input and contributions to their lives.

Azer Mahmood

He is a Peterborough born British-Pakistani man who has lived in Central Ward all his life. He was educated at the local primary and secondary schools.

Azer used PYA's youth facilities whilst growing up in the city. Several years later, Azer became a full time Youth Worker covering the Gladstone Area. During his work with young people in the community for many years and the young people admired, respected and liked his calm style and laid-back attitude.

Since leaving, the Youth Services Azer has been running a successful business with multimillion pounds annual turnover and creating employment for many other local young people of the community.

Mohammed Sarfraz

He arrived in Peterborough from the Mirpur city at a very young age. He was educated in local primary and secondary schools and grew up in the Central Ward of the city.

As a young man, Sarfraz used the Asian Youth Club facilities, time to time helped as a volunteer and later became founding members of the Pakistan Youth Association. In early 2000, he worked as a youth worker for about five years. Young people liked in interaction skills, caring attributes and appreciated his involvement in their lives..

Sarfraz continues to reside in the city and work for the Peterborough Regional College as Learning Involvement & Diversity Advisor.

Dr Ayyaz Kauser

He is a Peterborough born British-Pakistani man. He was educated at the local primary and the secondary schools and grew up in the Central Ward of the city.

Dr Kauser was a member of the Asian Youth Club and regularly used the facilities. After qualifying as an MBBS doctor, he was appointed Chairman of PYA. Young people held him in high regard and viewed him as a professional man and a positive role model for the young people of the community. Dr Kauser works in local practices as a General Practitioner and continues to reside in the city.

Hafiz Musaddaq Shaheen

He is a Peterborough born British-Pakistani man. He grew up in Central Ward. He was educated at the local primary and secondary schools.

Musaddaq was interested in religious studies from a young age and memorised the entire Holy Qur'an. He has been in contact with members of the PYA by dropping in and holding discussions with young people as well as undertaking mentoring work with young people in schools via YMCA.

The young people view his guidance and involvement with appreciation especially with strong religious emphasis. Musaddaq continues to reside in the Central Ward of the city.

Nassar Khalil

He is a Peterborough born British-Pakistani man. He was educated at the local primary and secondary Schools and grew up in the Central Ward of the city.

After qualifying and practicing as a lawyer, Nassar maintained his contacts with the PYA by being a Positive Role Model, guest speaker speaking extensively about his growing up experience the community and career success, which inspired many young people.

Nassar's solicitor company is based in Peterborough and he continues to reside in the city.

Moving Forward

Being positive role models of young people means that the young people view these individuals as the community figureheads and young people champions, who understand their issues, concerns as well as being equipped with knowledge, and possess inspirational attributes. The nature of their advice will help guide and discipline young people.

Role models have the responsibility to continue setting high standards in their ideals and endeavour to sustain their contacts with young people. They should readily make themselves available by providing them with advice support and assistance when required to build young people's capacities.

My Role Models

The person who played the most important role in shaping my life was my late mother Azmat Jan. She was a caring and loving person with had strong religious beliefs. From an early age, she taught me the differences between right and wrong and she always put strong emphasis on honesty, truthfulness and morality.

I was close to my mother and she had great confidence in my ability to resolve any difficult situation. I truly believe that it was my mother's prayers and the will of Allah, which helped me to achieve successes in my life.

The second person to influence my early life was my maternal grandfather the late Haji Babu Mohammed Ibrahim. He was a confident, well-educated, knowledgeable, and pious man.

Grandfather was a Petition Writer by profession and based in the Mirpur City court building, where he provided advice on legal, family and civilian matters – writing official petitions on behalf of the people.

At the age of 16, he voluntarily led Friday prayers at our village mosque and led Eid Prayers for several surrounding villages.

Grandfather was a great believer in education and I clearly recall from my early childhood memories that he encouraged me to study hard. His words still echoes in my ear:

"Education is the key to prosperity in life".

Life of Quaid-e-Azam Muhammad Ali Jinnah

He is known in Pakistan as Quaid-e-Azam "Great Leader" and Baba-e-Qaum "Father of the Nation" Muhammad Ali Jinnah the founder of Pakistan was born on 25th December 1876 into a prosperous Gujarati merchant family from the state of Gondal situated in the Kathiawar region province of Gujrat.

At the age of 16 Quaid-e-Azam passed the matriculation examination of the University of Bombay. In 1892, Quaid-e-Azam was offered an apprenticeship at the London office of Graham's Shipping and Trading Company in London. Quaid-e-Azam soon left the apprenticeship to study law instead at Lincoln's Inn. In three years at age 19, he became the youngest Indian to be called to the bar in England.

In 1896, Quaid-e-Azam returned to India and settled in Bombay and built a house in Malabar Hill, later known as Jinnah House. He became a successful lawyer, gaining particular fame for his skilled handling of cases.

In September 1913, Quaid-e-Azam became the president of the All-India Muslim League until Pakistan's independence on 14 August 1947. He was Pakistan's first Governor-General.

In September 1923, he was elected as Muslim member for Bombay in the new Central Legislative Assembly.

On 11th August 1947, Quaid-e-Azam expressed his views in a policy speech on Pakistan and said:

"There is no other solution. Now what shall we do? Now, if we want to make this great State of Pakistan happy and prosperous, we should wholly and solely concentrate on the well-being of the people, and especially of the masses and the poor. If you will work in co-operation, forgetting the past, burying the hatchet, you are bound to succeed. If you change your past and work together in a spirit that everyone of you, no matter to what community he belongs, no matter what relations he had with you in the past, no matter what is his colour, caste or creed, is first, second and last a citizen of this State with equal rights, privileges, and obligations, there will be no end to the progress you will make. I cannot emphasize it too much. We should begin to work in that spirit and in course of time all these angularities of the majority and minority communities, the Hindu community and the Muslim community, because even as regards Muslims you have Pathans, Punjabis, Shias, Sunnis and so on, and among the Hindus you have Brahmins, Vashnavas, Khatris, also Bengalis, Madrasis and so on, will vanish. Indeed if you ask me, this has been the biggest hindrance in the way of India to attain the freedom and independence and but for this we would have been free people long long ago. No power can hold another nation and specially a nation of 400 million souls in subjection; nobody could have conquered you, and even if it had happened, nobody could have continued its hold on you for any length of time, but for this. Therefore, we must learn a lesson from this. You are free; you are free to go to your temples, you are free to go to your mosques or to any other place or worship in this State of Pakistan. You may belong to any religion or caste or creed that has nothing to do with the business of the State. As you know, history shows that in England, conditions, some time ago, were much worse than those prevailing in India today. The Roman Catholics and the Protestants persecuted each other. Even now, there are some States in existence where there are discriminations made and bars imposed against a particular class. Thank God, we are not starting in those days. We are starting in the days where there is no discrimination, no distinction between one community and another, no discrimination between one caste or creed and another. We are starting with this fundamental principle that we are all citizens and equal citizens of one State. The people of England in course of time had to face the realities of the situation and had to discharge the responsibilities and burdens placed upon them by the government of their country and they went through that fire step by step. Today, you might say with justice that Roman Catholics and Protestants do not exist; what exists now is that every man is a citizen, an equal citizen of Great Britain and they are all members of the Nation. Now I think we should keep that in front of us as our ideal and you will find that in course of time Hindus would cease to be Hindus and Muslims would cease to be Muslims, not in the religious sense, because that is the personal faith of each individual, but in the political sense as citizens of the State"

On 11th October 1947, Quaid-e-Azam address to Civil, Naval, Military and Air Force Officers in Karachi and he said:

"We should have a State in which we could live and breathe as free men and which we could develop according to our own lights and culture and where principles of Islamic social justice could find free play".

Quaid-e-Azam Muhammad Ali Jinnah the founder of Pakistan

On 21st of February 1948, Quaid-e-Azam in an address to the sixth Light Regiments in Karachi said:

"You have to stand guard over the development and maintenance of Islamic democracy, Islamic social justice and the equality of manhood in your own native soil. With faith, discipline and selfless devotion to duty, there is nothing worthwhile that you cannot achieve".

On 11th September 1948 at 10.20 pm Quaid-e-Azam died at the Governor-General's House in Karachi at the age of 71 years and just over a year after Pakistan's independence, Quaid-e-Azam was buried in Karachi. His funeral was followed by the construction of a massive mausoleum, Mazar-e-Quaid, in Karachi to honour him; official and military ceremonies are hosted there on special occasions.

Sir Dr Allama Muhammad Iqbal

Sir Dr Muhammad Iqbal was born on 9th November 1877 in Sialkot. He was a Muslim poet and philosopher whose poetry in Urdu and Persian is considered to be amongst the greatest of the modern era.

After studying in England and Germany, Iqbal established a law practice, but concentrated primarily on writing scholarly works on politics, economics, history, philosophy and religion. He is best known for his poetic works, including Asrar-e-Khudi which brought a Knighthood, Rumuz-e-Bekhudi, and the Bang-e-Dara with its enduring patriotic song Tarana-e-Hind. In Afghanistan and Iran, where he is known as Iqbal of Lahore, he is highly regarded for his Persian works.

Allama Iqbal was a strong proponent of the political and spiritual revival of the Islamic civilisation across the world. He is known as "The thinker of Pakistan" and the "Poet of the East". He is officially recognised as the "national poet" in Pakistan.

After suffering for months from illness, Iqbal died in Lahore on 21st April 1938. His tomb is located in Hazuri Bagh the enclosed garden between the entrance of the Badshahi Mosque and the Lahore Fort. Official guards are maintained there by the Government of Pakistan.

Sir Dr Allama Muhammad Iqbal the National Poet of Pakistan

The Heritage of the Community

Community Activists

Introduction

The community activists are individuals who have played a significant role within the Peterborough British-Pakistani community by giving their time and commitment, as well as making valuable voluntary contributions in various capacities. I strongly feel that these people truly deserve the recognition and I consider them as the champions and the backbone of the community for over 50 years. This is my acknowledgement for their involvement in the development of the Peterborough British-Pakistani community.

Inclusion

The list is in alphabetical order and some of those listed activists have since deceased but the fruits of their excellent work live on as a memory. This heritage book is inclusive of all activists. I have listed a maximum of two positions against each name, although I am aware that many activists' contributions were/are much greater.

Councillors are not included under this heading as they are people elected representatives with much broader roles and responsibilities.

Apology

I am covering a timeline dating back from the past half-century, and regardless of the amount of research I conduct, I am still likely to miss out someone, please accept my sincere apology for excluding your name. I have recognised the following community activists:

- *Abdul Aziz*
  Treasurer of the Pakistan Welfare Association

- *Abdul Aziz*
  Treasurer of Ghousia Mosque Committee

- *A T Bashir*
  Treasurer of the Pakistan Welfare Association

- *Abdullah Abdul Majid*
  Secretary of the Pakistan Welfare Association and Secretary of the Gladstone District Community Association

- *Abdul Malik Chaudhari*
  Vice President of the Pakistan Welfare Association

- *Abdul Muqaddas Choudhuri*
  President of the Faizan-e-Madinah Mosque Committee and
  President of Pakistan Welfare Association

- *Abdul Ghani*
  Secretary Jamia Mosque Committee

- *Abdul Qayyum Malik*
  Secretary of the Pakistan Welfare Association

- *Ashfaq Hussain*
  Secretary of the Pakistan Community Association

- *Azam Tahir (deceased)*
  President of Pakistan Kashmir Welfare Association

- *Bashir Ahmed*
  President of the UK Islamic Mission

- *Babu Mohammed Yousaf*
  Chairman of the Youth Education Committee and Chairman of the
  Gladstone District Community Association

- *Chaudhry Arshad Ahmed (deceased)*
  Chairman of Ghousia Mosque Committee and Chairman of the
  Pakistan Welfare Association

- *Chaudhry Mohammed Aurangzeb (deceased)*
  Secretary of the Jamia Mosque Committee

- *Dr Ayyaz Kauser*
  Chairman of Pakistan Youth Association

- *Fateh Alam*
  Chairman of Ghousia Mosque Committee

- *Ghulam Sabir Choudhry (deceased)*
  Secretary of the Pakistan Welfare Association and Secretary of the
  Asian Community Association

⅄ *Ghulam Shabbir*
Chairman of the Pakistan Community Association and Chairman of the Asian Youth Club

⅄ *Ghulam Yousaf Kayani (deceased)*
Chairman of the British Pakistan Welfare Association

⅄ *Habib ur Rahman*
Treasurer of the Pakistan Community Association and Treasurer of the Faizan-e-Madinah Mosque Committee

⅄ *Hafiz Abdul Malik (deceased)*
President of the UK Islamic Mission

⅄ *Haji Babu Fazal Hussain (deceased)*
Secretary Pakistan National Association

⅄ *Haji Fazal Karim (deceased)*
Chairman of the Jamia Mosque Committee

⅄ *Haji Fazal Karim*
Chairman of the Jamia Mosque Committee

⅄ *Haji Ghulam Din*
Chairman of Ghousia Mosque Committee

⅄ *Hafiz Mohammed Asif*
Secretary of the Faizan-e-Madinah Mosque Committee

⅄ *Haji Mahmood Quereshi*
Secretary of the Jamia Mosque Committee

⅄ *Haji Mardan Ali (deceased)*
Chairman of the Jamia Mosque committee

⅄ *Haji Mir Baz Khan*
Treasurer of the Jamia Mosque Committee

⅄ *Haji Mohammed Suleman*
Vice President of the Pakistan National Association

⅄ *Haji Sawar Khan*
Treasurer of the Jamia Mosque Committee

⅄ *Haq Nawaz*

Chairman of the Pakistan Community Association

⋏ *Idris Akhtar*
Chairman of the Pakistan Community Association

⋏ *Javed Mirza*
Chairman of the Gladstone Community Association

⋏ *Haji Karamat Hussain – President (deceased)*
Chairman of the Pakistan Community Association and President of Pakistani National Association

⋏ *Khalid Sayed*
Chairman of the Pakistan Community Association

⋏ *Khurshid Lodhi (deceased)*
Treasurer of the UK Islamic Mission

⋏ *Mirza Nasir Ahmed*
Chairman Jamia Mosque Committee

⋏ *Mohammed Afzal*
Treasurer of the Gladstone District Community Association

⋏ *Mohammed Amin*
Secretary of Ghousia Mosque Committee

⋏ *Mohammed Aslam Inqauilabi*
Secretary of the Jamia Mosque Committee

⋏ *Mohammed Aurangzeb*
President of the UK Islamic Mission

⋏ *Mohammed Ayub*
Secretary Asian Youth Club

⋏ *Mohammed Latif*
Treasurer Jamia Mosque Committee

⋏ *Chaudhry Maqbool Hussain (deceased)*
Chairman of the Jamia Mosque Committee

⋏ *Mohammed Rashid*
Secretary of Pakistan Youth Association

- *Mohammed Sarfraz*
  Secretary of the Pakistan Community Association

- *Mohammed Sarwar Rija*
  Treasurer of the Pakistan Community Association and President Pakistan Welfare Association

- Mohammed Tariq
  Treasurer of Pakistan Youth Association

- *Mohammed Yousaf Malik*
  Chairman of Beeches School Governing Committee

- *Mohammed Younis*
  Secretary of the Faizan-e-Madinah Mosque Committee

- *Mohammed Younis*
  Chairman of the Dar Assalaam Mosque Committee

- *Munawar Khan*
  Chairman of Ghousia Mosque Committee

- *Muzzafar Hussain*
  President of the UK Islamic Mission

- *Nasir Mahmood (deceased)*
  Secretary of Ghousia Mosque Committee

- *Naseer Sethi*
  Chairman of the Gladstone Community Association

- *Pervez Khan*
  Chairman of Pakistan Youth Association

- *Raja Ghazanfar Ali*
  Chairman of the Faizan-e-Madinah Mosque Committee and Vice Chairman of the Pakistan Community Association

- *Raja Rashid Ahmed (deceased)*
  Chairman of Neighbourhood House Committee

- *Raja Tahir Masood*
  Vice Chairman of Beeches School Governing Committee

- *Salim Alhussain Alwi*
  Secretary of the UK Islamic Mission

- *Sajjad Ali*
  Secretary of Pakistan Youth Association

- *Shahid Hussain*
  Secretary of the Pakistan Community Association

- *Shabir Akhtar*
  Chairman of the Gladstone District Community Association

- *Riaz Shahid*
  Secretary of the Jamia Mosque Committee

- *Shabir Ahmed*
  Secretary Pakistan Youth Association

- *Tassaddiq Hussain*
  President of the UK Islamic Mission

- *Zahore Rahman*
  Secretary of the Dar Assalaam Mosque Committee

- *Zulifiqar Ali*
  Secretary of the Pakistan Community Association

National Monument of Pakistan in Islamabad - Construction started in
May 2004 and completed in March 2007

The Heritage of the Community

Peterborough Personalities

Community Personality

Habib-ur-Rahman also known as Billy was born in the district of Mirpur in Azad Jammu and Kashmir, Pakistan. His family was relocated at the time of Mangla Dam building to the district of Jhelum in Punjab Pakistan.

Habib arrived in Peterborough at the age of eleven and attended a local secondary school. During his school days, he was an athlete and in his teenage years a skilful amateur boxer. After leaving school, he completed an apprenticeship in "Croft Engineering" at Baker Perkins and was an employee of the firm for 20 years.

Habib has been a community activist for over 20 years, being involved from youth committee to community association and from mosque committee to NHS.

I describe Habib as a well known and a very unique individual.

Young Personality

Zain Haider Awan is a Peterborough born 17-year-old British-Pakistani man who attended both local primary and secondary schools. From a young age, Zain has been passionate about politics and leadership. The highlights of his involvement are:

- Peterborough Youth Council.
- Part of the UK Youth Parliament.
- Debated in the House of Commons Chamber for the National UK Youth Parliament debate.
- Vice chair of Hussaini Youth.
- Volunteer for the Interfaith Council of Peterborough.
- Head of public relations of the Peterborough Youth Council.
- Passionate about tackling discriminations faced by the Black and Minority Ethnic Communities.
- Set up Beyond Boundaries, a Government funded project
- Been part of various consultations around young people who face inequalities.
- One of the three UK Young Ambassadors from the UK Youth Parliament.

- ◆ Attended a conference in Hungary and represented the UK for the European Presidency and met with a Chinese Delegation.
- ◆ Working on a project with the UK Youth Parliament and Plan UK to developing youth parliament structures in Zimbabwe and Pakistan.
- ◆ Awarded one of the most prestigious awards – The Malcolm X Young Person of the Year.
- ◆ Awarded the Young Person of the Year award.
- ◆ He is a recognised young advocate for the community.

I describe Zain a vibrant, enthusiastic young man who will achieve even greater successes in his adult life.

Shalamar Gardens in Lahore constructed by Mughal Emperor Shah Jahan in 1642 - UNESCO World Heritage Site

Kaghan valley in Pakistan

The Heritage of the Community

Inspirational Quotes

Below are inspirational humanitarian, religious, political, educational, equality, wisdom, humorous, motivational, visionary, war, peace, work, truthful and life quotes. I hope you will find them as inspiring and motivating as I have in my life.

- The ink of the scholar is more sacred than the blood of the martyr.
- Say what is true, although it may be bitter and displeasing to people.
- Kindness is a mark of faith, and whoever is not kind has no faith.
- Happy is the person who finds fault with himself instead of finding fault with others.
- Power consists not in being able to strike another, but in being able to control oneself when anger arises.

Prophet Muhammad (PBUH)

- Run away from greatness and greatness will follow you.
- A wise man first thinks and then speaks and a fool speaks first and then thinks.

Hazrat Ali ibn-e-Abi Talib (RA)

- There is greatness in the fear of God, contentment in faith of God, and honour in humility.

***Hazrat Abu Baker* Sadique (RA)**

- The person I like most is the one who points out my defects.

Hazrat Umar ibn al-Khattab (RA)

- Exhorted people to acquire two habits namely: the habit of speaking the truth; the habit of doing good deeds.

Hazrat Usman Ghani (RA)

- If you are truthful, you will survive. If you lie, you shall perish.
- The earth destroys its fools, but the intelligent destroy the earth.

Khalid ibn al-Waleed.

- Come forward as servants of Islam organise the people economically, socially, educationally and politically and I am sure that you will be a power that will be accepted by everybody.

♯ Islam expect every Muslim to do this duty, and if we realise our responsibility time will come soon when we shall justify ourselves worthy of a glorious past.

♯ Expect the best, Prepare for the worst.

Quaid-e-Azam Muhammad Ali Jinnah

♯ I learned that courage was not the absence of fear, but the triumph over it. The brave man is not he who does not feel afraid, but he who conquers that fear.

♯ There is no easy walk to freedom anywhere, and many of us will have to pass through the valley of the shadow of death again and again before we reach the mountaintop of our desires.

♯ Let freedom reign. The sun never set on so glorious a human achievement.

Nelson Mandela

♯ I believe in the religion of Islam. I believe in Allah and peace.

♯ He who is not courageous enough to take risks will accomplish nothing in life.

♯ We have one life; it soon will be past; what we do for God is all that will last.

Muhammad Ali (boxer)

♯ Freedom is never voluntarily given by the oppressor; it must be demanded by the oppressed.

♯ Our lives begin to end the day we become silent about things that matter.

♯ Almost always, the creative dedicated minority has made the world better.

Dr. Martin Luther King Jr

♯ Without education, you are not going anywhere in this world.

♯ The future belongs to those who prepare for it today.

♯ You are not supposed to be so blind with patriotism that you cannot face reality. Wrong is wrong, no matter who says it.

Malcolm x also known as El-Hajj Malik El-Shabazz

- Education is the best provision for the journey to old age.

Aristotle

- Nations are born in the hearts of poets; they prosper and die in the hands of politicians.
- Destiny is the prison and chain of the ignorant. Understand that destiny like the water of the Nile: Water before the faithful, blood before the unbeliever.

Sir Dr Allama Muhammad Iqbal

- It is easy to be human, very hard to be humane.

Mirza Ghalib

- We now have the enemy in front of us and the deep sea behind us. We cannot return to our homes, because we have burnt our boats. We shall now either defeat the enemy and win or die a coward's death by drowning in the sea.

Tariq ibn Zayad

- Do not impose on others what you yourself do not desire.
- Everything has beauty, but not everyone sees it.

Confucius

- Loneliness is the most terrible poverty.
- If you cannot feed a hundred people, then feed just one.
- Intense love does not measure it just gives.

Mother Teresa

- Ignorance is the mother of poverty.
- What we are not ashamed to do before God, we should not fear to do before our fellowmen.
- When a nation becomes devoid of arts and learning, it invites poverty. And when poverty comes it brings in its wake thousands of crimes.

Sir Syed Ahmad Khan

- One-day life of tiger is better than 100 years life of jackal.

Tipu Sultan

- An ounce of practice is worth more than tons of preaching.
- Those who know how to think need no teachers.

Mohandas Gandhi

- Never in the field of human conflict was so much owed by so many to so few.
- I have nothing to offer but blood, toil, tears and sweat.

Sir Winston Churchill

- Courage is knowing what not to fear.

Plato

- A nation, which makes the final sacrifice for life and freedom, is not beaten.

Mustafa Kemal Ataturk

- Efforts and courage are not enough without purpose and direction.

John F. Kennedy

- Racism is still with us. But it is up to us to prepare our children for what they have to meet, and, hopefully, we shall overcome.

Rosa Parks

- Yes, you have to sing from the depths of the heart.

Nusrat F. A. Khan

- I wanted to be an outstanding player that was my ambition.

Imran Khan

- A revolution is a struggle to the death between the future and the past.

Che Guevara

- Let the beauty of what you love be what you do. *Rumi*

Author's late father Haji Anayat Ali and late Haji Mohammed Fazil, one of the earliest arrivals in Peterborough

The Heritage of the Community

Abdul Rahman, the first British-Pakistani Special Constable in the 1960s in Peterborough

The Heritage of the Community

Author's late Uncle Raja Abdul Majid LLB was the
first graduate to have arrived in Peterborough

Memorable picture of late Chaudhry Noor Mohammed
and his son Chaudhry Mohammed Rashid in the 1980's

The Heritage of the Community

A memorable picture of late Haji Fazal Karim the
former Chairman of Jamia Mosque

The Heritage of the Community

A Prominent Community Activists, the late Chaudhry Arshad Ahmed

A Renowned Scholar the late Hafiz Abdul Malik Sahib

The Heritage of the Community

Late Haji Fazal Karim and Beloved Personality
the late Moalna Mustafa Sahib

The Heritage of the Community

Late Malik Khadim Hussain with his son, Ghulam Shabbir Awan in the 1960

The Peterborough British-Pakistani Community early Pioneer
the late Chaudhry Mohammed Aurangzeb

Late Haji Karamat Hussain the first
President of Pakistan National Association

The Heritage of the Community

Memorable Pictures of late Chaudhry Muhammed
Sarwar one of the earliest arrivals in the city 1957/8

Author, Raja Tahir Masood, Cllr Mohammed Azad, Ansar Ali and
Mohammed Sabir

The Heritage of the Community

محمود ہاشمی ۔ علی گڑھ ۔ 1943

Mahmood Hashmi a Renowned Academic

Muhammad Zafran Awan in the 1960s

The Heritage of the Community

Late Chaudhry Maqbool Hussain
the former Chairman of Jamia Mosque

Leading Community Activist late Ghulam Yousaf Kayani

The Heritage of the Community

Malik Muhammad Saqlain in the 1960s

The Heritage of the Community

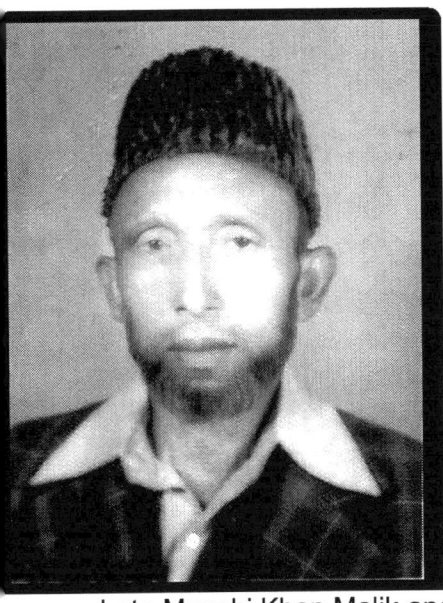

Late Munshi Khan Malik and Abdul Qayyum Malik in 1980s

Late Mohammed Ismail of village Morah Bari in 1960's

The Heritage of the Community

Ansar Ali, Raja Tahir Masood, Councillor Nazim Khan MBE, late Dr Ayub Thakur a Prominent Kashmiri figure and Raja Akhtar Hussain Raja
in 1980's

Raja Skandar Khan, (positive role model) Mohammed Nadim and Mohammed Sabir in 1988

Raja Tahir Masood, Ansar Ali, Arshad Mahmood and Raja Akhtar
Hussain Raja introducing Halal food at the Gladstone Primary School in
the early 1990s

Mohammed Sabir and Habib-ur-Rahman in 1992

The Heritage of the Community

Councillor Nazim Khan MBE with David Miliband Foreign British
Secretary with Mohammed Sabir and Abdul Majid

First summer school success at Ghousia Mosque facilitated by their
former Secretary Ansar Ali

The Heritage of the Community

A memorable picture of the Author, Raja Tahir Masood

The Heritage of the Community

Muzaffar-ul-Hassan after Pak Azad cricket team winning the Cup and with rest of the team

Author, Raja Tahir Masood on a weeklong residential
at the Isle of Weight

Author, Raja Tahir Masood Presenting his Autobiography to former
Glasgow Govan MP Mohammed Sarwar (the first British Muslim MP)
on 5th October 2011 at Peterborough

The Heritage of the Community

Young people in Gladstone Street, c1980s

Children in the Gladstone Area in late 1970,s

The Heritage of the Community

Author, Raja Tahir Masood with young people on a residential at the
Isle of Weight

Pakistan Youth Association Members

Young People at the Peterborough United Football Match

The Heritage of the Community

References

I thank following people and the organisations for their sources of information.

- Abdullah Abdul Majid: Pakistan Welfare Association and Faizan-e-Madinah Mosque.

- Abdul Rahman: Early city arrival experience and first British-Pakistani community graduate.

- Abdul Razaq: Involvement in the community prior and after elected Councillor.

- Abdul Qayyum Malik: Pakistan Welfare Association, generally about Kotli and Mirpur districts

- Asian Youth Club Members: Positive role models.

- Ansar Ali: Ghousia Mosque, Asian Youth Club, community involvement prior and after elected Councillor and the community activists.

- British Broadcasting Corporation (BBC): Cousin Marriages.

- CD Porsz: Gladstone children pictures.

- Dungarwalla/Tayabali families: Dawoodi Bohra Muslim Association.

- Ghulam Shabbir: Burton Street Mosque, Pakistan Community Association, Asian Youth Club and Zain Awan.

- Internet Sites: Migration history, Immigration legislations, Anti-discrimination acts, population data about different town, cities, districts, statically data's on the British-Pakistani Community and various reports.

- Haji Mohammed Suleman: Early arrival experience, 110 Russell Street and the Pakistan National Association.

- Haji Sabir Hussain: Late father Chaudhry Rahmat Khan.

- Khalid Mahmood Junvee: Consenting to usage of late Chaudhry Fakeer Mohammed picture and general support.

- Karim Bhai: Shia Imma Nizari Ismaili community.

- Mahmood Fazal: Community involvement.

- Mohammad Ayub Choudhary: Involvement in the Community prior and after elected Councillor and achievements whilst serving as a Mayor.

- ✓ Mohammed Jamil: Father Mohammed Hussain and their involvements in the community prior and after elected Councillors.

- ✓ Mohammed Nazir: First arrival experience in the city.

- ✓ Mohammed Sabeel: Involvement in the community prior - after elected Councillor, the Gladstone Park and current job.

- ✓ Mohammed Younis: Faizan-e-Madinah Mosque and the community activists.

- ✓ Muzaffar-ul-Hassan: Pak Azad cricket team.

- ✓ Muzaffar Hussain: Masjid Khadijah Islamic Centre and the Community activists.

- ✓ Nazim Khan MBE: Involvement in the community prior and after elected Councillor.

- ✓ National Reports: British-Pakistani community.

- ✓ Pakistan Youth Association Members: Positive role models.

- ✓ Peterborough City Council: Black & minority and the new Communities arrival Children, Kay stage results, relevant educational acts applied to Black and minority pupils.

- ✓ Peterborough Evening Telegraph: Educational National league tables and the Peterborough position.

- ✓ Peterborough City Council Member Services: Councillors and Mayors and the Deputy Mayors

- ✓ Peterborough City Council Link Officer: city links worldwide.

- ✓ Raja Akhtar Hussain Raja: Involvement in the community prior and after elected Councillor and achievements whilst serving as a Mayor

- ✓ Raja Ghazanfar Ali: Faizan-e-Madinah Mosque and community involvements.

- ✓ Shahid Anwar: The Sarai Alamgir community.

- ✓ Tanveer Hussain: Late father Chaudhry Muhammed Sarwar.

- ✓ The Muslim News Paper: Reports relating to British Muslim communities.

- ✓ Zahore Rahman: Dar Assalaam Mosque and the community activists

Raja Tahir Masood - Author's Profile

I was born in a small village of Morah Bari in the district of Mirpur in Azad Jammu and Kashmir, Pakistan.

I migrated to Britain at the age of 14 with my family and Peterborough has been my home for over 30 years.

I was employed full time by Peterborough City Council and Cross Keys Homes in various officer positions for about 20 years.

My community related involvement and experiences;

✓ Former executive committee member of several community and District Associations.

✓ Primary and secondary school governor, member of County Council Education Appeals and youth patch Committees.

✓ Current local government district branch Executive Committee Officer for over 20 years and hold the positions of the Equality and International Officer.

✓ Member of the Eastern Region UNISON Black members committee for over 20 years and Chairperson for over 10 years.

✓ Treasurer of the British Friends of Islamgarh Welfare Trust national charity.

✓ Youth Worker with young people for about 30 years.

The Heritage of the Community